LIMITED LIABILITY COMPANIES MADE E-Z!

E·Z LEGAL FORMS®

Deerfield Beach, Florida
www.e-zlegal.com

Limited Liability Companies Made E-Z™
Copyright 1999 E-Z Legal Forms, Inc.
Printed in the United States of America

E·Z LEGAL FORMS®

384 South Military Trail Deerfield Beach, FL 33442
Tel. 954-480-8933 Fax 954-480-8906
http://www.e-zlegal.com/
All rights reserved.
Distributed by E-Z Legal Forms, Inc.

1 2 3 4 5 6 7 8 9 10   CPC   R 10 9 8 7 6 5 4 3 2

This publication is designed to provide accurate and authoritative information in regard to subject matter covered. It is sold with the understanding that neither the publisher nor author is engaged in rendering legal, accounting, or other professional services. If legal advice or other expert assistance is required, the services of a competent professional should be sought. From: *A Declaration of Principles jointly adopted by a Committee of the American Bar Association and a Committee of Publishers.*

Limited Liability Companies Made E-Z™

Important Notice

Limited warranty and disclaimer

This self-help legal product is intended to be used by the consumer for his/her own benefit. It may not be reproduced in whole or in part, resold or used for commercial purposes without written permission from the publisher. In addition to copyright violations, the unauthorized reproduction and use of this product to benefit a second party may be considered the unauthorized practice of law.

This product is designed to provide authoritative and accurate information in regard to the subject matter covered. However, the accuracy of the information is not guaranteed, as laws and regulations may change or be subject to differing interpretations. Consequently, you may be responsible for following alternative procedures, or using material or forms different from those supplied with this product. It is strongly advised that you examine the laws of your state before acting upon any of the material contained in this product.

As with any legal matter, common sense should determine whether you need the assistance of an attorney. We urge you to consult with an attorney, qualified estate planner, or tax professional, or to seek any other relevant expert advice whenever substantial sums of money are involved, you doubt the suitability of the product you have purchased, or if there is anything about the product that you do not understand including its adequacy to protect you. Even if you are completely satisfied with this product, we encourage you to have your attorney review it.

It is understood that by using this guide, you are acting as your own attorney. Neither the author, publisher, distributor nor retailer are engaged in rendering legal, accounting or other professional services. Accordingly, the publisher, author, distributor and retailer shall have neither liability nor responsibility to any party for any loss or damage caused or alleged to be caused by the use of this product.

Copyright Notice

The purchaser of this guide is hereby authorized to reproduce in any form or by any means, electronic or mechanical, including photocopying, all forms and documents contained in this guide, provided it is for nonprofit, educational or private use. Such reproduction requires no further permission from the publisher and/or payment of any permission fee.

The reproduction of any form or document in any other publication intended for sale is prohibited without the written permission of the publisher. Publication for nonprofit use should provide proper attribution to E-Z Legal Forms.

Money-back guarantee

E-Z Legal Forms offers you a limited guarantee. If you consider this product to be defective or in any way unsuitable you may return this product to us within 30 days from date of purchase for a full refund of the list or purchase price, whichever is lower. This return must be accompanied by a dated and itemized sales receipt. In no event shall our liability—or the liability of any retailer—exceed the purchase price of the product. Use of this product constitutes acceptance of these terms.

Table of contents

This product does not constitute the rendering of legal advice or services. This product is intended for informational use only and is not a substitute for legal advice. State laws vary, so consult an attorney on all legal matters. This product was not prepared by a person licensed to practice law in this state.

5

How to use this guide

E-Z Legal's Made E-Z™ Guides can help you achieve an important legal objective conveniently, efficiently and economically. But it is important to properly use this guide if you are to avoid later difficulties.

◆ Carefully read all information, warnings and disclaimers concerning the legal forms in this guide. If after thorough examination you decide that you have circumstances that are not covered by the forms in this guide, or you do not feel confident about preparing your own documents, consult an attorney.

◆ Complete each blank on each legal form. Do not skip over inapplicable blanks or lines intended to be completed. If the blank is inapplicable, mark "N/A" or "None" or use a dash. This shows you have not overlooked the item.

◆ Always use pen or type on legal documents—never use pencil.

◆ Avoid erasures and "cross-outs" on final documents. Use photocopies of each document as worksheets, or as final copies. All documents submitted to the court must be printed on one side only.

◆ Correspondence forms may be reproduced on your own letterhead if you prefer.

◆ Whenever legal documents are to be executed by a partnership or corporation, the signatory should designate his or her title.

◆ It is important to remember that on legal contracts or agreements between parties all terms and conditions must be clearly stated. Provisions may not be enforceable unless in writing. All parties to the agreement should receive a copy.

◆ Instructions contained in this guide are for your benefit and protection, so follow them closely.

◆ You will find a glossary of useful terms at the end of this guide. Refer to this glossary if you encounter unfamiliar terms.

◆ Always keep legal documents in a safe place and in a location known to your spouse, family, personal representative or attorney.

Introduction to Limited Liability Companies Made E-Z™

The limited liability company, commonly referred to as an LLC, has quickly become one of the most popular business entities in the United States. Once seen as a daring corporate hybrid, the LLC is now praised for its organizational flexibility and innovation. It combines the best features of corporate protection with the significant tax advantages of a partnership.

While it is no longer a new type of company, many business professionals including attorneys and accountants are not familiar with its basic purpose and structure nor its advantages over traditional business forms such as the corporation, partnership and sole proprietorship. Some experts predict the LLC will eventually replace partnerships and corporations as the preferred method of doing business.

For tax reporting purposes, the Internal Revenue Service recognizes LLCs as partnerships. Yet, they are not partnerships, since LLCs provide limited liability to members. Like a corporation, personal assets are protected from debts and other obligations incurred by the business. Yet, they are not corporations. And, unlike both partnerships and corporations, all members of a limited liability company may participate in the management of the company. These are the three primary advantages of the LLC.

The potential of the LLC has already made it the choice of thousands of entrepreneurs, and the list is growing every year. As you read this guide, you'll see why the LLC might be the choice for *your* business!

What type of business is right for you?

1

Chapter 1

What type of business is right for you?

Is an LLC right for you?

There are four basic forms of business entities: the individual or sole proprietorship, the partnership, the corporation and the limited liability company. Each has unique characteristics and abilities, and choosing the right form of business involves many considerations. Important factors used to determine the type of business entity you wish to use include:

- liability and personal exposure

- costs, including filing fees and tax considerations

- the available methods of raising capital

- the ability to attract and keep key personnel through various fringe benefits or participations such as stock options

- the time and costs of conversion

The LLC is the newest type of business entity, but it may not be the right choice for you. To get an idea of what form of business will best work for you, let's examine the advantages and disadvantages of the other three more traditional types of business.

> *note*
>
> The greatest advantage of a limited liability company is that it has the tax advantages of a partnership and the limited liability of a corporation.

The sole proprietorship

The sole proprietorship is the simplest form of business organization. It is a business owned by an individual who is solely responsible for all aspects of the business. The owner is personally responsible for all debts of the business, even in excess of the amount invested. The business and its owner are thus considered the same entity.

The advantages of a sole proprietorship include:

1) low start-up costs, because legal and filing fees are at a minimum. However, many states and cities require at least a filing with the county clerk, especially if a fictitious business name is adopted.

2) greatest freedom from regulation and paperwork

3) owner is in direct control with no interference from other owners

4) taxes may be lower than with corporations

The disadvantages include:

1) unlimited liability. The proprietor is responsible for the full amount of business debts no matter how incurred, which means that his personal property may be taken to cover debts of the business. This, of course, is a significant disadvantage.

2) unstable business life, since the sole owner's death or illness would terminate the business

3) difficulty in raising capital or obtaining long-term financing because you cannot readily sell an ownership interest in a sole proprietorship

The partnership

A partnership is a legal entity that is jointly owned by two or more individuals (although in some cases partners may also be corporations or other entities). As with the sole proprietorship, the owners are personally liable for all debts of the firm, unless a limited partnership is set up.

Limited partnerships are complex legal structures, and one partner, known as the general partner, still must have unlimited liability. Even agreements for regular partnerships can be quite complex.

The advantages of a partnership include:

1) low start-up costs—since there usually are fewer filing fees and franchise taxes

note Each year, a partnership must file an annual report with the IRS. The report must show the earnings and losses and the partner's share of that profit or loss. Annual reports can be simple to elaborate and are often used as marketing tools.

2) a broader management base than a sole proprietorship, and a more flexible management structure than a corporation

3) possible tax advantages—because a partnership avoids the double taxation of corporations and because income can be taxed at personal income rates. However, the personal income situations of the partners could also make this a disadvantage.

4) availability of additional sources of capital and leverage by adding limited and special partners

5) the duration of the entity can be limited to a stated time, or may continue indefinitely by amendment

The disadvantages include:

1) unlimited liability of at least one partner (in a limited partnership) and possibly all partners (in a regular partnership). Personal assets of the general partners are available to satisfy partnership debts.

2) the life of a partnership is unstable, since the addition or departure of partners causes the partnership to terminate

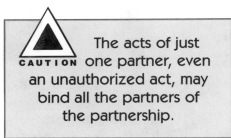
CAUTION The acts of just one partner, even an unauthorized act, may bind all the partners of the partnership.

3) obtaining large sums of capital is relatively difficult, since financing cannot be obtained from the public through a stock offering, as in a corporation

4) an individual partnership interest cannot be sold or transferred easily

5) most tax-supported fringe benefits, such as pension and profit-sharing arrangements, are unavailable to partnerships

A partnership may be formed for a single, isolated purpose and then dissolved. For example, developers may form a partnership to build a single planned unit community and then dissolve the partnership and turn the property over to its owners for further daily management.

One important distinction between a general partner and a limited partner—liability. A limited partner is not personally liable for partnership debts. A limited partner, at most, loses the amount actually or agreed to be paid into the partnership. This capital contribution or the amount received should the partnership become insolvent, are the only possible losses for a limited partner.

The corporation

A corporation is formed and authorized by law to act as a single entity, although it may be owned by one or more persons. It is legally endowed with rights and responsibilities and has a life of its own independent of the owners and operators. It has been defined by the United States Supreme Court as "an artificial being, invisible, intangible and existing only in contemplation of the law." Think of it as a distinct and independent entity separate from its owners.

Unlike a sole proprietorship or partnership, the corporation continues to exist even if an owner (shareholder) dies or sells his shares of the business. In addition, personal liability is limited and owners share the burden only to the extent of their investment in company shares.

The advantages of a corporation include:

DEFINITION

1) *limited liability*. The owners are not personally liable for debts and obligations of the corporation. They can personally lose only to the extent of their investment in the corporation, with the exception that they may be personally liable for certain types of taxes, such as payroll taxes withheld from the employees' paychecks but not paid

to the Internal Revenue Service and state tax authorities. If the business fails or loses a lawsuit, the general creditors cannot attach the owners' homes, cars and other personal property. Limited liability is one major reason so many businesses are incorporated.

2) capital can be raised more easily than under other forms of ownership. This does not mean, however, that a new corporation can easily sell shares of stock. The sale of stock is highly regulated by both federal and state governments, and obtaining bank loans for a fledgling business may be no easier for a new corporation than for a partnership or proprietorship.

3) ownership in a corporation is more easily transferrable, including transferring shares to family members as well as selling your interest to another person. However, in many small corporations it is advisable

note A corporation has a defined, centralized management. Control rests in the board of directors and its powers are exercised through the officers.

to put restrictions on the transfer of shares, especially if the stockholders must be able to work together. This is generally accomplished by stockholder agreements.

4) since the corporation is an independent legal entity, it has a continuous existence. It does not cease simply because one of the owners dies or retires.

6) many companies offer discounts, in areas such as travel, to corporations

7) retirement funds, defined-contribution plans, money-purchase plans, and other profit-sharing, pension and stock option plans may be more easily set up with a corporation

The disadvantages include:

1)   corporations are the most expensive form of business to organize

2)   there is double taxation, since both the corporate entity and the individual owners have to file tax returns. (This may be avoided with a "Subchapter S" corporation.)

3)   record-keeping requirements can be more extensive with a corporation

 note Corporations are subject to more governmental regulations than either partnerships or sole proprietorships.

4)   operating across state lines can be complicated because corporations need to "qualify to do business" in states where they are not incorporated

5)   ending the corporate existence, and in many cases even changing the structure of the organization, can be more complicated and costly than for partnerships and proprietorships

If you decide that the corporation is the correct form of organization for your business, you must go through the legal steps required to create your corporation. These steps vary in complexity from state to state. With careful planning, most people can easily organize their own corporation without a lawyer, thus saving hundreds of dollars in legal fees. E-Z Legal's *Incorporation Made E-Z* helps take you through the procedures without a lawyer.

The S corporation

An S corporation is similar to a limited liability company in that, for tax purposes, it is treated like a partnership or sole proprietorship. An S corporation has the same structure as a regular C corporation, in that its shareholders own the corporation and elect a board of directors to oversee the daily policies and procedures. But, the S corporation has the added advantage of maintaining a pass-through tax status as in a partnership. Once you are incorporated, you must elect to switch to S corporation status and then file your change in status with the state.

As you will see, an S corporation sounds a lot like a limited liability company. However, there are a few differences that make the LLC the better choice for many types of business. Two main reasons why an LLC might be better is that it requires:

1) Less paperwork. There is much less paperwork required for an LLC compared to that of a corporation.

2) Lower start-up costs. Registering an LLC, as well as annual fees, are much lower than they are for a corporation. In addition, some types of corporations require a lawyer to set up; LLC's can be set up without an attorney or their expensive fees.

BUSINESS ENTITY COMPARISON CHART

TYPE OF ENTITY	SOLE PROPRIETOR.	GENERAL PARTNERSHIP	LIMITED PARTNERSHIP	C CORPORATION	S CORPORATION	LIMITED LIABILITY CO.
SIZE	One Person Ownership	Two or More Person Ownership	One or More Partners	Unlimited	Up to 75 Members	Minimum of One Member*
TAXATION	Once	Once	Once	Double	Once	Once
LIABILITY	Owner	General Partner(s)	Company	Corporate	Corporate	Company
START-UP	Easiest	Easy	Complex	Complex	Most Complex	Easy
DISSOLUTION	Easiest	Easy	Complex	Complex	Most Complex	Complex
BUSINESS EXAMPLE	Mom & Pop Candy Store	Home Builder	Professional Business	Public Corporation	Small Business	Any Type of Business

*Although some states recognize single-member LLCs, most states still require at least 2 members.

The limited liability company

2

Chapter 2

The limited liability company

What you'll find in this chapter:

- ⟶ How the LLC came to be
- ⟶ Advantages to creating an LLC
- ⟶ Disadvantages to creating an LLC
- ⟶ The Uniform Limited Liability Company Act
- ⟶ General provisions of an LLC

Origins of the LLC

The idea of the limited liability company is not new. It has existed for hundreds of years in Europe, where the first significant limited liability company law was passed in Germany in 1892. Many countries in both Europe and Latin America followed Germany's lead, and the late 1800s saw an outgrowth of these companies in the United States. Called "partnership associations," they were similar to present LLCs, providing basic liability protection for members. But they were never very popular in the United States—even though they continued to be the dominant business entity in Europe—partly because the legislation here was considered too restrictive.

It wasn't until 1977 that the state of Wyoming passed special legislation recognizing the LLC. This legislation was designed to lure a large Texas oil company (previously doing business as an LLC in Panama) to Wyoming. The IRS reacted to this legislation in 1980 by declaring that since personal liability of members of the LLC was limited, it could not be granted the same favorable tax status currently enjoyed by partnerships. Five years later, in an effort to attract more business, Florida followed suit with similar legislation, but there was too much uncertainty regarding the IRS for LLCs to really develop. And, without favorable tax status, the advantages of the LLC were too limited to spark solid interest or growth.

> *note* Federal tax regulations and state laws controlling how an LLC is created and taxed are still evolving. But the trend is toward easing restrictions and allowing greater flexibility.

The big impetus came in 1988 when the IRS reversed its previous stance and passed ruling 88-76, which granted special tax status to LLCs. This ruling opened the door for any state to consider its own legislation and many did. Today, all states recognize LLCs.

Advantages of an LLC

A limited liability company combines the advantages of a corporation with those of a partnership. There are many reasons why it may be your business form of choice:

1) double taxation is avoided. Since it is not a corporation, there is no corporate income tax. Income is only taxed on the personal level, as in a partnership.

2) personal liability is limited. All the personal assets of the partners are protected from corporate creditors. Managers and officers are also protected if they participate in the operation of the company.

3) there is relatively little paperwork and record keeping beyond a simple operating agreement or statement of the principles of the organization

4) you can form a limited liability company yourself. The forms are available from the Secretary of State of the state in which you want to form the company. You do not need an attorney.

5) you can convert your present business to a limited liability company and begin receiving the benefits immediately

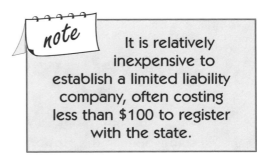

note It is relatively inexpensive to establish a limited liability company, often costing less than $100 to register with the state.

6) annual registration fees are low, under $150 in most states

Disadvantages of an LLC

Although an excellent choice, the LLC is not necessarily for everyone. Reasons to choose forming a corporation or partnership instead include:

1) there is still a lack of widespread acceptance of the LLC because this type of company is relatively new. Limited liability companies have been recognized by the IRS only since 1988.

2) multi-state businesses may have tax problems if they conduct business in a state that does not yet recognize limited liability companies, or if the LLC fails to qualify to do business in another state

3) IRS rules that apply to insolvency may create problems for the owners of the limited liability company

4)   limited liability companies do not enjoy the advantages of IRS rulings when there is a sale of worthless stock or stock is sold at a loss

CAUTION Limited liability companies may not engage in tax-free reorganizations.

5)   the sale of 50% or more of the ownership of the limited liability company in any 12-month period ends any tax advantages the company may have had with the IRS

General provisions of an LLC

Although some state statutes vary, most conform to the model established by the Uniform Limited Liability Company Act (ULLCA) of 1995. This Act was drafted by a panel of scholars and attorneys. While neither state nor federal law, it is the most comprehensive treatment available on the subject of LLCs and contains guidelines that most states refer to and adopt regarding LLCs.

Here are some general provisions of the ULLCA:

1)   an LLC has a legal identity separate from its members

Definition:

Members. The owners or shareholders of the LLC.

2)   an LLC may be organized for profit or for non-profit

3)   in about half of the states, an LLC may have only one member; the balance require at least two members

4)   LLC property interest is non-transferable

5)   interest in distribution and return of capital can be transferable

6) members of an LLC do possess limited liability

7) managers are agents of the company and have authority to bind the company to third parties

8) an LLC may exist for a fixed or perpetual duration

9) an LLC is dissolved upon:

Definition:
Operating Agreement. Similar to by-laws of a corporation, these are rules adopted by an LLC that detail the company's operating procedures.

    a) the consent of members

    b) the dissociation of a member

    c) the occurrence of a specific event described in the operating agreement

10) members may freely transfer their rights to distributions but not their rights to membership. An LLC grants the right to membership only upon the vote of the remaining membership.

11) the LLC Operating Agreement may not:

    a) unreasonably restrict a member's right to inspect company records

    b) eliminate or reduce a member's duty or loyalty, care or good faith dealings with and to the company

    c) restrict the rights of third parties

    d) override the legal right of the company to expel any member convicted of wrongdoing, breaching the Operating Agreement, or making it impractical for the LLC to carry on business with such a member

Naming your LLC

Chapter 3
Naming your LLC

Once you are ready to set up your own LLC, you must first select a company name and check to see if the state in which you are going to register will allow you to use the name.

Names you can't use

It isn't as easy as just finding the right name, since the state has to approve the name you choose. The first obstacle, other than your own originality, will be the state statutes, which prohibit the use of certain words. Not all states have the same prohibitions, so you should check the laws of your particular state.

However, words that typically cannot be used include:

Acceptance	Endowment	Pharmacy
Architect	Engineering	Savings
Bank	Federal	State Police
Banking	Guaranty	Thrift
Board of Trade	Indemnity	Trust
Certified Accountant	Insurance	United States
Chamber of Commerce	Lawyer	Urban Relocation
	Loan	Underwriter
Cooperative	Medical	Urban Development
Credit Union	Mortgage	
Doctor	National	

These words are, of course, used in the names of organizations or corporations whose types of business require special licensing or regulation. Such businesses must be organized pursuant to statutes regulating their particular fields. It is not advisable to attempt to set up such a company without the assistance of a lawyer.

Names you must use

note

When considering your company name, also check what must be included in the name. All states require that an LLC's name include an indication of limited liability, so that people dealing with the organization know that if it fails, they cannot collect their debts from the owners personally. Each state has specific wording and/or abbreviations you can choose from, and these may include the following:

Limited Liability Company	L.L.C.
Limited Company	Limited Co.
Ltd. Company	L.C.
LLC	Ltd. Co.

This requirement should be checked carefully before selecting the name, as each state will allow only certain wording. See the Appendix for the requirements for your state.

Choosing a name

Once you've decided on a name, you must investigate whether the name you want is already being used by someone else, whether used by a corporation, a partnership, or another LLC. Even similar names can cause problems, because most states will not allow a name that is the same or "deceptively similar" to a name already on record in the state. Therefore, your XYZ Ltd. Co. restaurant may be a problem, for example, if there is already an XYZ Inc. bakery in the state.

When you file your LLC name you:

- ensure that you don't use another business' name

- ensure that another business doesn't take your business name

- provide a public identification for your business to help avoid any possible confusion with others

One useful thing to keep in mind is to choose a descriptive word along with a proper name for your LLC. Perhaps XYZ Foods Ltd, or XYZ Restaurant LLC., in the above example, would be accepted, whereas XYZ Ltd. Co. might be refused on the basis of its being "deceptively similar" to the XYZ, Inc. already in existence.

note Keep in mind that many states charge a separate fee for reserving a company name in addition to a registration filing fee.

The materials you obtain from the Secretary of State will help you learn how to reserve the name. Usually it is done by submitting a letter or a form with the required fee and waiting to receive clearance. In some cases you can check the availability of the name with a telephone call. Always clear the proposed corporate name before you prepare and file your corporate papers.

Where to register your LLC

4

Chapter 4

Where to register your LLC

The next step in forming your limited liability company is to decide where to register your company. It would seem obvious to register in the state where you are located, but there may be advantages to registering in another state. There are two main types of factors to consider: financial and organizational.

Financial factors

Filing fees and annual recording fees vary considerably between the states; it could cost as little as $10 or as much as $2,000 to set up your LLC, depending on where you register. Taxes are also an important consideration, which we will discuss in a moment.

When considering the financial factors involved in registering your LLC, ask yourself the following questions:

- What are the costs of registering in the state where your physical facilities are located?

- If you register in another state, what will it cost to become authorized to do business in the first state?

- What are the fees to check and reserve your company name?

- Will you be charged a one-time state entity tax? This is often based upon the number of shares authorized for the company to issue.

- Will you be charged annual fees? These may include a filing fee for an annual report or an annual franchise tax.

- Will you be charged state or local income taxes? If so, how are they determined?

Organizational factors

State laws governing the organization of LLCs can be another important factor. When considering in which state to register, also weigh state-by-state differences in these areas:

- Is management of the company by members or an appointed manager?

- May LLCs merge with other forms of business?

- Who has power to bind the company and act as its agent(s)?

- How easily may company members be admitted and withdrawn?

• What are the standards of negligence, malfeasance, misfeasance, misconduct, confidence, trust and confidentiality?

Bulletproof vs. flexible

For tax purposes, the IRS recognizes LLCs as partnerships. Not all states, however, have adopted the same rulings, so you need to look at the statutes regarding tax status in the state you wish to register. At this time, LLCs can be categorized with three types of status based on state statues that deal with the formation and taxation of a limited liability company:

1) *Bulletproof.* If state statutes follow the IRS guidelines, the LLC is taxed as a partnership and the statutes are referred to as "bulletproof."

note

If you set up your company in a bullet-proof state, you have no choice but to follow their laws of formation so you will qualify for partnership tax status.

note As of the publishing date of this guide, Florida, Minnesota, Nebraska, Nevada, South Dakota, Virginia, and West Virginia are the only states which have "bulletproof" statutes.

2) *Flexible.* Some states have enacted laws which allow too much organizational flexibility. These statutes are "flexible," as opposed to "bulletproof" states where there are no options. This is not to say you cannot qualify for partnership tax in "flexible" states as well, but you must choose that state's correct, qualifying organizational options.

3) *Flexible-bulletproof.* A third type of statute is referred to as "flexible-bulletproof." These statutes contain default rules that if followed, lead to partnership tax classification. However, they also allow sufficient modification by members of an LLC, to jeopardize the company's partnership tax status.

There have been many IRS rulings since 1977 that continue to define and establish guidelines for forming and operating an LLC, and some would argue that IRS rulings become more liberal with time. Nevertheless, the issues are constantly evolving.

The American Bar Association and the American Conference of Commissioners on Uniform State Laws have drafted models upon which states may base their laws. This attempt to simplify and unify the laws has met with little success. While many similarities do exist from state-to-state, significant differences still abound.

The foreign LLC

Another factor to consider when registering your LLC is where your primary business will take place. You could register in a state with lower fees, such as New Mexico, but if most of your business is done in another state you may have problems. If you register in a state other than the one in which you intend to do business, you may be forced to register as a "foreign" LLC under the foreign corporation statute of your primary business state. This can lead to a significant increase in filing, registration and administration costs.

If your business is, for example, going to be a retail store in Hartford Connecticut and you register your LLC in New Mexico, you would still have to qualify "to do business" in Connecticut. The advantages of New Mexico registration would have to be very great to overcome the burden for most small businesses of being subject to regulation by two states. If you plan to do business outside your company's state of registration, you may have to qualify as a foreign LLC in every state where you do business. You would then need to consider the registration factors for each of those states, as well as pay all the fees for each.

Make certain that you do register in another state if you will indeed be doing business in that state.

⚠ **CAUTION** If you are doing business in another state but have not qualified by filing the proper papers and paying the fees, the consequences can be serious.

In all states, an unqualified "foreign LLC" is denied access to the courts of the state, which would mean you could not sue someone in that state to enforce a contract or obligation. In addition, in many states fines are imposed by the state when it discovers an LLC doing business there without having qualified, and in some cases members, managers or agents may be subject to these fines. In extreme cases, the LLC may be forced to dissolve.

"Doing business"

DEFINITION

So just what constitutes "doing business" in a state? The statutes of many states define what "doing business" is. While engaging in interstate commerce by itself does not constitute "doing business," if you engage in such interstate commerce and have a registered office, address or agent in a state other than the one in which you registered initially, you need to register in that state as a foreign LLC. Other principal business activities considered "doing business" are:

- soliciting and receiving orders by mail within that state

- soliciting orders within that state through an agent, sales representative or independent contractor

- shipping orders from a warehouse within that state

- paying state taxes

- accepting service of process

Since requirements vary from state to state, you should consult the statutes in any state in which you contemplate one or more of the above activities.

The Model Corporation Act

The Model Corporation Act, drafted by a group of lawyers and law professors, gives a list of activities which, in and of themselves, do *not* constitute "doing business." Since this act is the basis for corporate laws in many states, and since it can be applied to LLCs, it is a good guide to what you can do *without* having to qualify as a foreign LLC. The language reads:

Without excluding other activities which may not constitute transacting business in this state, a foreign corporation [LLC] shall not be considered to be transacting business in this state, for the purposes of this Act, by reason of carrying on in this state any one or more of the following activities:

1)   maintaining or defending any action or suit or any administrative or arbitration proceeding, or effecting the settlement thereof or the settlement of claims or disputes

2)   holding meetings of its directors or shareholders or carrying on other activities concerning its internal affairs

3)   maintaining bank accounts

4)   maintaining offices or agencies for the transfer, exchange and registration of its securities or appointing and maintaining trustees or depositories with relation to its securities

5)   effecting sales through independent contractors

6) *soliciting or procuring orders, whether by mail or through employees or agents or otherwise, where such orders require acceptance without this state before becoming binding contracts*

7) *creating as borrower or lender, or acquiring indebtedness or mortgages or other security interests in real or personal property*

8) *securing or collecting debts or enforcing any rights in property securing the same*

9) *transacting any business involved with interstate commerce*

10) *conducting an isolated transaction that is completed within a period of 30 days which is not in the course of a number of repeated transactions of like nature*

 In other words, any of these things can be done by a foreign LLC and it will not be viewed as doing business in that state. If you do have to become authorized to do business as a foreign LLC, the procedure is relatively simple. Obtain the Articles of Organization designed for a foreign LLC from the Secretary of State of the state in which you want to qualify, complete it and file it with the proper fees.

The Articles of Organization

5

Chapter 5

The Articles of Organization

What you'll find in this chapter:

- ➤ What Articles of Organization will do
- ➤ Who may file the Articles
- ➤ Choosing when to file
- ➤ The different parts of the Articles
- ➤ Amending your Articles

---

note

Once you decide where you will register, your next step is to file the Articles of Organization. Using state-provided forms will speed up the process and help avoid costly errors. Return them to the office of the Secretary of State or the state's Department of Corporations where you obtain your state's forms (see the Appendix). Additionally, some states require that a public notice of intent be published in a general circulation newspaper.

By filing the Articles of Organization, you serve notice on all third parties that your company is an LLC and that it is in compliance with, and abides by, all terms and conditions of the law.

note
Some state statutes actually require you to include their governing laws, with either the citation or language, in your Articles of Organization.

Who may file

Some states require that the Articles of Organization be filed by a person called an "organizer" who is not an officer, director or stockholder in the company. Other states require the organizer to be a "natural person," a member of the company or a business entity. This person names the initial manager in the Articles. Upon application to the state, you will receive the necessary information to begin the filing process including the filing fees. You will also be notified who may file the Articles.

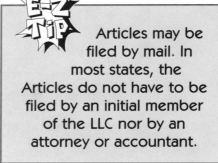

Articles may be filed by mail. In most states, the Articles do not have to be filed by an initial member of the LLC nor by an attorney or accountant.

When your LLC is born

The business will be shielded with limited liability only when the state issues a Certificate of Organization. Try to obtain two copies of the completed forms as evidence of the LLC's anniversary date. Depending on the state, this date can be when the Articles of Organization were signed, submitted or approved, or on a date specified by state statute.

There are four possible anniversary dates of an LLC depending upon the state it is registered in:

1) on the actual date the Articles of Organization were signed

2) on the date the Articles were submitted to the State

3) on the date the Articles were officially approved

4) on a specific date specified by state statute

Drafting the Articles of Organization

While most states provide forms for the purpose of drafting the Articles of Organization, some only provide guidelines or send non-returnable sample forms. Since you may also want to include additional information in your Articles beyond the space allotted in the form, use the following as a guide.

Generally, Articles of Organization include:

- **Name of the company.** The name must follow the guidelines as discussed in Chapter 3 of this guide, and must be cleared and reserved with the state in which you are registering.

- **Statement of purpose.** Great care should be taken when stating the intended purpose of the proposed LLC.

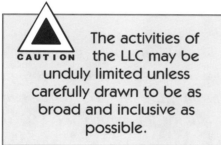

CAUTION — The activities of the LLC may be unduly limited unless carefully drawn to be as broad and inclusive as possible.

When the powers granted the company are not broad enough for its needs, the LLC must petition the state to "amend" its Articles of Organization before it may expand its activities beyond those originally approved.

To draft appropriate purposes and activities for the LLC, follow these two steps:

1) Write down a statement setting forth the specific objectives, purposes, and activities the LLC will engage in, including all related lines of business. For example, in a construction business, the statement of purpose might be written as follows:

Purposes: To engage in the construction, repair and remodeling of buildings and public works of all kinds, and for the improvement of real estate, and the doing of any other business and contracting work incidental to or connected with such work, including demolition.

A general merchandising business might write the following statement of purpose:

Purposes: To manufacture, produce, purchase or otherwise acquire, sell, import, export, distribute and deal in goods, wares, services, merchandise and materials of any kind and description.

Always add the following statement to allow for future contingencies and to protect the right of the company to expand its future activities:

The foregoing purposes and activities will be interpreted as examples only and not as limitations, and nothing therein shall be deemed as prohibiting the LLC from engaging in any lawful act or activity for which an LLC may be organized under the laws of _____ (name of state).

- **Address of the company.** Include both mailing and street address where records are kept.

- **Statement of duration.** As a partnership and not a corporation, an LLC does not have a perpetual life separate from its members. Thirty years from inception generally is designated as the last date on which the LLC will do business and wind up its affairs.

- **Name and address of the registered agent.** All states require the LLC to have a registered agent. This person, whether a member or not, will receive important legal documents such as service of process and tax information.

If your business is physically located in the state of registration, the company itself, or an officer, would be the registered agent. If you register in a state where you do not actually have an office, you need a local agent. Organizations that represent companies for a small annual fee can be found in law directories.

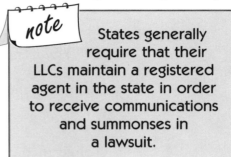

States generally require that their LLCs maintain a registered agent in the state in order to receive communications and summonses in a lawsuit.

- **Membership.** This statement affirms that the LLC consists of at least two persons or parties, where required, in order to constitute a partnership.

- **Rights of members.** These rights deal with admitting new members and continuing operations after the incapacity or withdrawal of any one member.

- **Other provisions.** This includes optional terms such as restrictions on authority.

- **Authorized signature.** Signature of person authorized to execute the Articles of Organization.

Amending the Articles

If any significant information changes or if defects are found in the Articles of Organization, state law often requires amending the Articles and submitting a formal notice to the Secretary of State.

State law often requires the Articles of Organization be amended if any of the following occur:

- a change in the number of members or managers

- a change in the stated purpose or name of the company

- a member's withdrawal

- a change in the registered agent

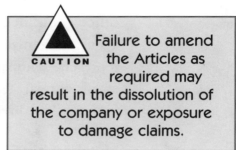
CAUTION Failure to amend the Articles as required may result in the dissolution of the company or exposure to damage claims.

- a change in the company's registered address

- a defect in the Articles of Organization is discovered

The Organizational Meeting

6

Chapter 6
The Organizational Meeting

What you'll find in this chapter:

➠ Creating your Operating Agreement

➠ Bank accounts and transferring assets

➠ Applying to the IRS and your fiscal year

➠ Records and meetings

➠ State and local requirements

As soon as the state approves the Articles of Organization, the company must hold its Organizational Meeting. This first meeting will take care of some very important set-up activities necessary for the running of your LLC, as well as establish the tone for which you will be doing business.

There are nine main items that will be on the agenda of your Organizational Meeting:

1) Creating your Operating Agreement

The most important thing to accomplish at this meeting is to propose and adopt the Operating Agreement. This document outlines the rules and procedures, or operating requirements, for running your LLC, and in most states it is required to be kept as part of your records. Later, the Operating Agreement and these requirements will be explained in more detail.

---

2) Electing your managers

A limited liability company is run by a manager or managers, chosen by the members. Most often the LLC managers are members of the company, though it is not a requirement. Each state has default rules regarding the management of an LLC.

3) Establishing bank accounts

To open a company bank account, you need an Employer Identification Number for your LLC (see #5 below). Another item probably required by the bank is a "company resolution," a duly signed statement that serves as an official company indication of authorization to open such an account(s).

4) Transferring assets to the LLC

Whether or not you have been operating a business prior to LLC registration (as many people do), you can transfer your assets and debts, or the assets and debts of the prior business, to the new LLC at an agreed sum or for other consideration and receive shares in exchange. You cannot, however, burden the company with more debts than assets.

Assets transferred to the LLC do not necessarily have to be monetary; they can also be personal, real or intangible property. You should keep an account of your asset transfers using the appropriate documents found in this guide:

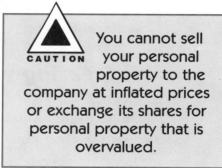

You cannot sell your personal property to the company at inflated prices or exchange its shares for personal property that is overvalued.

- *Bill of Sale*, for the transfer of personal property (tangible property except real estate)

- *Quitclaim Deed*, for the transfer of real property (real estate)

- *Assignment of Assets*, for the transfer of intangible property (such as licenses, stocks and bonds, copyrights, trademarks, patents, promissory notes and franchises)

It is sound business practice to notify all existing business associates, creditors and customers or clients of the change to an LLC status. This can be done by personal communication (telephone or letter), or by a small newspaper notice. Generally, all subsequent company records and transactions should be changed to reflect the new LLC status of the organization, including the printing of new letterheads, business cards, stationery and signage.

5) Applying to the IRS

Once your Certificate of Organization has been filed and approved, you need to apply for an employer identification number by completing and returning form SS-4 to the IRS. If you already have an employer identification number for a Keogh Plan account, or because you have had employees prior to registering as an LLC, you nevertheless need a new number for the LLC, as the LLC is a new entity.

6) Choosing a fiscal year

You will note that the IRS Request for Employer Identification Number asks for your fiscal year. In some states even the Certificate of Organization requires the fiscal year to be given. Of course, it is easiest to choose the calendar year as your company's fiscal year. You will have fewer tax forms to file that way. However, if that is undesirable, a second choice would be July 1 to June 30.

The advantage of a separate fiscal year is that it allows flexibility in tax planning. By having two tax years to work with, you and your accountant have more flexibility in tax planning. And the tax savings, company and personal, can be significant.

7) Establishing records

You may want to choose a fiscal year on the advice of your accountant, who can determine the fiscal year most advantageous to you.

At this first meeting, you must implement record keeping procedures, including taking minutes of the Organizational Meeting.

Remember that your LLC is viewed in the eyes of the law as a different "legal entity," separate and apart from the owner(s). Hence, to avoid potential IRS problems, you must maintain separate sets of records, one for your personal affairs and one for the affairs of the LLC. As a rule, however, it is not necessary to maintain an elaborate bookkeeping system. A separate bank account and bookkeeping that clearly show what you and the LLC separately earn and pay out is usually sufficient. A local bookkeeper or accountant can easily set up a convenient accounting and tax system for your business.

8) Determining state and local requirements

Beyond the formalities of registering an LLC, other regulations and requirements must also be considered. Permits and licenses, for example, are required for such businesses as:

Many businesses, such as brokerage and securities businesses, air transportation, banking and drug manufacturing companies, are regulated by federal agencies. Before commencing any new business, consider what regulations are applicable so that your business will not be in violation.

In addition, any business that hires employees must consider whether or not it:

- is subject to withholding taxes for local, state and the federal government

- whether it must pay social security tax, unemployment insurance or workers' compensation

- whether unions have jurisdiction and what pension or other payments must be made to them

Be aware of minimum wage requirements, the permissibility of hiring minors, and any occupational safety and health regulations. A helpful resource for any employer is the E-Z Legal's *Employment Law Made E-Z*.

Counseling sponsored by the Service Corps of Retired Executives (SCORE) is extremely helpful, and they may offer free on-site counseling services, and free workshops and seminars.

The Small Business Administration of the federal government was established by Congress in 1953 to assist small businesses. This agency provides prospective, new and established members of the small business community with financial and management training and counseling. Check your Yellow Pages for their local office.

Also contact your local trade associations and the local chamber of commerce. They, too, can give you advice and assistance.

9) Establishing the time and place of successive meetings

Not every state requires regular meetings and meeting minutes be kept in the official company record. However, it is always a good idea to keep your business as organized as possible and to keep lines of communication open among your members.

The Operating Agreement

7

Chapter 7
The Operating Agreement

Members of the LLC enter into an Operating Agreement that spells out the economic and management arrangements as well as other rights and obligations of the members of the LLC. Operating Agreements may be extremely flexible, allowing members a wide range of options as to how the company will be run and problems solved. However, it is important not to include anything in the Agreement that might jeopardize tax status.

The operating requirements

1) **Articles of Organization.** Most of the information included in the Articles of Organization such as the name, address, duration, registered office and agent are included in the Operating Agreement.

2) **Voting rules.**

- Will a majority or unanimous vote be necessary to take action, or will it depend upon the nature of the action?

> *note* Your Operating Agreement must determine what is the voting power of members, if any.

- Can members or managers vote outside of meetings?

- Is vote by proxy or conference call allowed?

- In what manner will votes be cast: will votes be per capita, by contribution or by some other method?

3) **Amendments.** Procedures for amending the Operating Agreement are outlined. Under what conditions will a vote be taken for amendment?

4) **Recordkeeping** and accounting practices. This will usually include:

- a current list of members and managers and their addresses

- copies of all the LLC tax returns for at least three years

- copies of all financial statements

- copies of the Articles of Organization and all amendments

- copies of any information relating to members financial contributions to the company

- accounting procedures to be followed

- how often reports will be made to members, if at all

5)   **Management.**

- Will the LLC be managed by members?

- What if any, are the necessary qualifications for management?

- How will managers be elected?

- Who will be the managing members?

- How long will the term of office be?

- What authority does management have and what specific limitations are placed on that authority when, for example, they deal with third parties or with each other?

- Who will keep the company records?

- How will managers be paid?

- How will successor managers be chosen?

- When and how can a manager be removed or resign from office?

> *note*
> Your Operating Agreement must determine what voting power management has as well as when and where may it be exercised.

6)   **Standard of care.**

- What standard of care must management and members exercise?

- What constitutes gross negligence, malfeasance, misfeasance or intentional misconduct?

- What is the standard of loyalty to the company?

7) **Members liability**. How are members to be indemnified if at all, when sued?

8) **Contributions.**

   • What constitutes a member's contribution to the company?

   • May contributions be in the form of cash, property, services or promises to deliver such?

   • Will members be obligated to make future contributions to meet future needs of the company?

9) **Distributions.** How will distributions among members be made, and under what conditions may distributions not be made, such as when insolvency occurs?

Along with these issues, there are a number of other items which can and should be addressed in the organizing of company procedures, such as:

   • How will profits and losses be allocated among members?

   • Under what conditions may a member resign or withdraw?

   • Under what conditions will dissolution occur?

   • How will managers and members be notified of meetings?

   • Will penalties be assessed for noncompliance?

   • How will vacation time be determined?

   • What type of insurance will the LLC carry?

   • In the event of a member's death, will the LLC buy-out the deceased's membership interest?

• How will the value of a deceased's membership interest be determined for buy-out purposes?

• To whom can a membership interest be transferred or sold?

 note Remember that most states require the Operating Agreement—and any subsequent amendments—to be in writing.

• How many signatures are required on a company check?

• How can the LLC obtain additional capital if it so requires?

• Should mandatory loans be required from the membership?

Initially, all members must agree to the Operating Agreement. Subsequent votes will be decided according to the voting terms outlined in the Operating Agreement. Even if your state does not require it, it would be wise to keep your records and procedures as accurate and clearly defined as possible.

Tax status of the LLC

Chapter 8

Tax status of the LLC

What you'll find in this chapter:

⟹ Choosing your IRS tax status

⟹ Characteristics of an LLC for tax purposes

⟹ Obtaining an IRS ruling on your tax status

⟹ Filing your LLC's tax returns

⟹ Accounting and tax shelters

The IRS checkbox

Choosing partnership or corporate status for federal tax filing purposes is now a matter of checking the appropriate box on IRS Form 8832 (Entity Classification Election). A January 1997 ruling created this simple check-box form. Now an unincorporated business is automatically (default rule) taxed as a partnership unless it checks the "corporation" box.

For now, determining your LLC's status for state income taxes is not quite as simple. Individual states are following suit with the recent IRS ruling and amend their LLC statutes accordingly. This would eliminate the possible confusion of LLCs being formed for partnership tax status under the new federal rules, yet being taxed as corporations by the state.

---

note   As of the printing of this guide, most state regulations are still structured around the former operating requirements for IRS partnership status.

To find out about any state's latest regulations and requirements, you must check with the attorney general's office in the state(s) where you plan to file (see the Appendix). Excepted from these new regulations would be:

note   For tax purposes, the IRS now recognizes single member LLCs, even though most states still do not.

- any publicly traded company

- corporations

- insurance companies and charities

- certain foreign-owned businesses

A single-owner business such as a sole proprietorship formerly had the option of being taxed as either a corporation or a sole proprietorship but not as a partnership. Now, under the new regulations, simply checking a box, entitles even single member LLCs to partnership tax status.

It is not clear exactly what impact the check-box system will have upon LLCs. Experts predict that if the IRS replaces its traditional six criteria test with a check-the-box system, most states will liberalize their LLC statutes and eliminate "bulletproof" statutes.

note   Default statutes would be unnecessary if the IRS accepts the checked box and investigates the company no further.

In addition, with a check-box system, the two member requirement for LLC formation would disappear. As the restrictive provisions of Operating Agreements disappear, LLCs can be tailored to meet real business needs without concern for IRS tax guidelines.

Companies would also be entitled to change their tax classification only once every five years, and the IRS says it will not question classifications for prior years. In other words, if a single member LLC elects to be taxed as a partnership, the IRS will not challenge its prior classification as an LLC.

Characteristics of an LLC

When creating your Operating Agreement and running your business, it is important to make sure that your LLC maintains the characteristics needed to comply with state/IRS tax requirements.

In order that the LLC be taxed as a partnership and not as an association or corporation, there must be strict adherence to state regulations governed by IRS Code section 7701(a)(3). The key to this code is the provision that an unincorporated organization, which the LLC certainly is, must have more noncorporate characteristics than corporate ones.

Under the Code, a theoretical corporation is defined by six "ideal" characteristics, which, when considered together, distinguish it from other business entities. These six characteristics are:

1) associates (there will be one or more persons participating in the business)

2) an objective to carry on business and divide the gains therefrom

3) continuity of life

4) centralized management

5) limited liability

6) free transferability of interests

Originally, a business entity that possessed no more than three of these characteristics qualified for partnership status for federal income tax purposes. If it possessed at least four, it was classified as a corporation.

However, since elements 1 and 2 are essential elements of every corporation and partnership, the IRS only focuses on the last four elements when considering an LLC. As long as no more than two of the last four elements are present, the LLC receives partnership tax status. These four elements are described in detail below.

Continuity of life

The IRS is concerned with the duration of the company and its essential relationship to its memberships. In general, LLCs do not have continuity of life (i.e., an unlimited or unspecified length of existence) as corporations do. A company does not have continuity of life if either:

◆ The company automatically dissolves following the death, resignation, expulsion, bankruptcy, insanity, appointment of guardian or conservator for, or retirement of, any of its members. This is not to say the company must dissolve after such an event, only that without a special provision in the Operating Agreement to the contrary, it would do so, or

Unlike a corporate charter, a special directive must be written into the Operating Agreement allowing the company to continue to exist by the consent of the members. This extra step prevents continuity of life while permitting continued existence. Without the additional action, the company would dissolve.

◆ There is a specified dissolution date; this is typically 30 years.

Centralized management

Since a corporation is generally managed by a board of directors and non-member shareholders have no management power, it is important that your LLC be managed by its members. Member-management means, however, that while every member has voting management authority, an executive board may be elected to run the company's daily affairs.

The important element the IRS looks for is the source of management's authority:

- Is management elected or appointed by the members?

- Does management have exclusive authority which does not need to be ratified by the members themselves?

> **note**
> By vesting management power in its members, an LLC can avoid the trap of centralized management.

If so, then it is centralized management.

It can be dangerous for an LLC to hire non-members as managers, even if not prohibited by state law. Before your LLC contemplates doing this, seek qualified legal counsel, otherwise your partnership tax status may be jeopardized.

Limited Liability

Limited liability is generally considered to be essential for all members of the LLC. Often, it is the very reason for forming an LLC. If this is so, then limited liability is not one of the elements you can use to define your tax status. In this respect there is no difference between an LLC and a corporation.

Some states do allow one member of the LLC to be personally liable for the debts and obligations of the company much in the same way a general partner is in a limited partnership. This person must have "substantial assets" that can be used to meet the obligations of the LLC. The IRS has defined "substantial assets" as at least 10 percent of the total capital in the LLC. He or she cannot be a mere figurehead. Such personal liability can

DEFINITION

note Limited liability does not extend to members who offer personal guarantees for leases, loans, and other legal documents.

be indemnified by another person because under local law, liability still exists.

note If you need to use this option in order to qualify for partnership tax status (you are willing to forsake limited liability) you must make it part of the Operating Agreement.

Free transferability of interests

A membership interest in an LLC, like personal property, can be assigned or transferred to a third party or pledged to a creditor. However, this does not mean that the assignee becomes a voting member of the LLC. The assignee may be entitled to receive distributions and a proportionate share of profits, but is not entitled to vote or participate in the management of the LLC.

note To be admitted into voting membership usually requires a unanimous vote of the existing membership or as otherwise spelled out in the Operating Agreement. This provision for voting on membership means that membership interests are not freely transferable.

note Since corporate shares may be freely transferred from one person to another, the LLC must not grant this.

Family-owned LLCs often take advantage of this limitation by placing restrictions upon to whom the membership may be transferred. For example, if transfers are restricted to members of the family, and a former spouse desires to dispose of membership, it must be transferred back to the family. In this sense the LLC can function as a prenuptial or antenuptial agreement.

> *note* Anyone assigning membership may then lose that membership for themselves.

Some states allow members to make prior transfer consent agreements. The IRS agrees such agreements do not jeopardize tax status as long as the right to share profits and not the authority to manage is being transferred.

Membership interests may be held in a variety of ways:

- *sole ownership*: there is only one owner

- *tenants-in-common:* two owners have the same interest in the membership property

- *joint tenancy with the right of survivorship*: two or more parties each own the entire membership property. Upon one party's death, the survivor may take the entire membership property

> **E-Z TIP** It is not recommended that ownership be held by tenancy by the entirety because this form of membership, similar to joint tenancy, has been abolished in many states.

Obtaining an IRS ruling

It is possible to obtain an IRS ruling on your LLC by mail. Although the procedure is complicated and expensive, you can resolve any doubts you have about the tax status of your LLC. Such a ruling gives your company the opportunity to comply before serious tax liability is incurred.

The fee for a Private Letter Ruling is about $500. It is based solely upon the information your company provides and applies only to your company. It does not address the LLC laws of your state. You must not use a prior ruling as a guide.

The fee for a written ruling ranges from $500 to almost $4000 depending upon the gross income of your company. Written rulings deal directly with state law. When a ruling is issued for a particular state, its text appears in the IRS Cumulative Bulletin. This bulletin is available in larger public libraries, law libraries and from the IRS itself.

 Rulings may be appealed, and information on the current tax status of a state usually can be obtained from a state's department of revenue.

Member contributions

Sometimes an investor offers to contribute property to the LLC in exchange for membership. Under the IRS Nonrecognition Rule, a member's contribution is considered of equal value to the membership interest. Therefore, no gain or loss is incurred and there are no tax consequences.

Exceptions to the Nonrecognition rule are:

1) If the member contributes services, the Nonrecognition Rule does not apply. Services are not considered property. In addition, any money or assets the member realizes from those services must be included in the member's gross income. Thus, there may be a taxable event.

2) If the member contributes property and receives assets or money in addition to membership status in the LLC, the IRS may treat the event as a sale with taxable consequences.

3)   If the member contributes property which is subject to debt and the debt exceeds the value of the property, a taxable gain is realized.

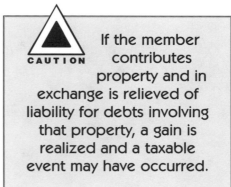

If the member contributes property and in exchange is relieved of liability for debts involving that property, a gain is realized and a taxable event may have occurred.

The IRS is very strict about gains or losses that result from contributions to an LLC. If you are considering such a contribution, seek counsel from a tax professional.

Filing tax forms

Although the LLC pays no taxes, its members are taxed as a partnership. Therefore, the LLC must file a partnership tax form. This form is known as form 1065. It is not strictly a tax form because it also provides information to the IRS about the LLC. There is a box in part B of the form that must be checked if the form is filled out by an LLC. Include the employer identification number as well. Additional schedules to fill out are:

- Schedule A of form 1065 is used by the LLC to report its income. The company lists the value of its inventory and the method it used to compute that value.

  The penalty for failure to file this form or filing an incomplete form is $50 times the number of members in the LLC.

- An LLC must also file a Schedule K-1 which shows money paid out as distributions. This form provides the IRS with information about members' income from the LLC.

- Schedule L is used to report the company's balance sheet

• Schedule D is used to report long-term (more than one year) and short-term (less than one year) capital gains and losses.

There may be additional schedules to file along with form 1065 if your LLC has:

- total gross receipts in excess of $250,000

- total assets in excess of $600,000

Tax matters are not unduly burdensome even for large LLCs. If the company is subject to a unified audit if it has any of the following:

- more than ten members

- a member who is not an individual (such as a corporation)

- a nonresident member

This simply means that the LLC is audited as a single business entity. The individual members are not normally subject to audit.

Accounting and tax shelters

Generally, every LLC has a choice of accounting methods. The two accepted methods are:

1) **Cash.** The cash accounting method derives company income from cash or property when actually received.

2) **Accrual.** The accrual method states that income is derived when the company receives the right to receive the cash or property.

While smaller LLCs generally use the cash method of accounting, the IRS requires the accrual method be used under two conditions:

1) If a C corporation with average annual income in excess of $5 million is a member of the LLC.

2) If the IRS determines the LLC to be a tax shelter. The three standard tests that determine tax shelter status are:

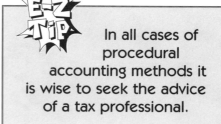 In all cases of procedural accounting methods it is wise to seek the advice of a tax professional.

a) The LLC offers membership interest(s) for sale and is required to register the offering with a state or federal agency.

b) The LLC was created principally to avoid paying taxes.

c) More than 35 percent of the company's losses are shared among or between limited partners. This is known as the syndicate test.

Specialized uses of the LLC

9

Chapter 9

Specialized uses of the LLC

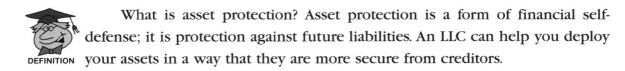

What you'll find in this chapter:

⟹ Asset protection with the LLC

⟹ Real estate advantages with the LLC

⟹ LLCs and foreign investors

⟹ The LLC as an estate planning tool

⟹ Using the LLC for charity fundraising

There are many ways to put the advantages of the LLC to special use. An LLC is particularly well suited for asset protection, real estate investment, foreign investors, estate planning, creditor transactions, multi-state operations, charitable organizations and professional practices.

Asset protection techniques

DEFINITION What is asset protection? Asset protection is a form of financial self-defense; it is protection against future liabilities. An LLC can help you deploy your assets in a way that they are more secure from creditors.

Business owners frequently start their venture as unincorporated sole proprietorships and become concerned about the possible loss of personal assets only as their business heads for bankruptcy. One answer to this problem is to quickly form an LLC and transfer the assets from the proprietorship into the new LLC. The new LLC should pay the oldest business obligations first. Since these would be obligations of the proprietorship for which you are personally liable, their discharge will free you of personal exposure.

As your LLC pays the older debts it will incur new debts, usually with the same suppliers. However, these debts are now those of the LLC since they were incurred after the LLC was organized. Eventually all proprietorship debts will be fully paid and your LLC can be safely liquidated as the creditors will have no further personal recourse against you. You

> *note*
> You must make sure your interest in the LLC is in another name so your personal creditors cannot take control of your company. Be an invisible member by legally concealing your membership interest from creditors.

note must be certain that your creditors apply your payments to the oldest balance—the proprietorship debts you want discharged. Note on each check how it is to be applied.

Another way to shield personal assets using an LLC is to owe the company money. The LLC may take a mortgage on your home, personal

> *E-Z TIP*
> In matters of divorce, an LLC may offer some additional asset protection. With an LLC a divorce-court judge would be unable to award ownership of the LLC stock to an ex-spouse who was not an original recipient.

property such as a car or boat, or even accept a "blanket" mortgage on all your property. Should you later run into personal problems, the mortgage held by your LLC can effectively insulate your personal assets from other creditors.

Alternatively, you may transfer each asset to a different LLC instead of transferring all assets to one LLC. The more owners there are of different assets, the harder it is for one creditor to link the assets and attach them. This insulates the remaining assets from being attached for the liability of one asset.

A single LLC can be divided into separate LLCs without risking dissolution of the original. Successor LLCs are consider to be a continuation of that original LLC if the members of the successor LLCs had at least a 50 percent interest in the prior LLC. The IRS considers this to be a restructuring, not a change in ownership.

Be careful about transferring all assets to an LLC. Many people use offshore LLCs and foreign trusts for this purpose. The trust conducts its affairs through an LLC. The trust then only owns this one asset, the entire interest of the LLC. This serves four important purposes:

1) the LLC can easily trade and do business through an operating company

2) the LLC insulates the trust from potential liabilities

> **note** The Bahamas, British Virgin Islands or Seychelles are common choices for tax havens because they are also strong privacy havens.

3) the LLC creates another layer of privacy

4) the LLC helps avoid U.S. income tax liability on most U.S. source investment income

The LLC is usually set up in a different tax haven than the trust haven, a country with favorable company laws.

The trustee usually serves as the manager of the LLC and manages the entire offshore system—the trust and the LLC—as one entity. It is actually the LLC owned by the trust that conducts these activities.

Do make transfers well before problems arise as courts will be most concerned about attempts to avoid your obligations. The key is not to wait until claims are made against you. Plan ahead, anticipate. If you make your transfers slowly, a little at a time, the conveyances are less likely to be deemed fraudulent and set aside by the courts.

Real estate investment

Traditionally, a limited partnership was set up to invest in real estate. However, the general partner still had unlimited liability exposure. So an S Corporation was set up as general partner. Because the general partner always had to have a net worth of at least 10 percent of the capital contributions of the limited partners, that 10 percent remained exposed. This is a cumbersome and very expensive entity, especially ill-suited for small real estate ownership.

note LLCs can be used effectively to replace the costly and burdensome need to set up a limited partnership, general partner and an S corporation to invest in real estate.

With the LLC, the 10 percent funding requirement and the need for two companies is completely eliminated. Since no assets remain exposed, the LLC also offers more liability protection. The LLC Operating Agreement can be used to provide additional capital for the project by requiring additional contributions from members as needed. NOTE: However, the Operating Agreement may also offer protection to its members by providing that no member shall be liable to the LLC, other members or third parties for failure to contribute.

LLCs also can be used in the same manner as are real estate investment trusts (REIT) and limited partnership syndications at far less cost and with less administrative complications.

Foreign investors

Foreign investors are often more familiar with LLCs than other American business entities. As mentioned earlier, LLCs have existed in Europe and Latin America for at least one hundred years. The advantage of using an LLC is that there are no statutory membership restrictions as there are in S corporations. S corporations are not allowed by law, to have nonresident aliens as shareholders. LLCs provide international investors with the same limited liability and pass-through tax status usually associated with S corporations.

Estate planning

Like the use of LLCs for real estate ownership, LLCs are ideal vehicles for transferring real estate investments as gifts to children. If the LLC owns the property, a membership interest in the LLC could be gifted instead of the property itself. Parents could retain managerial control of the LLC, receive compensation for services rendered and still be able to depreciate the gifts.

Two classes of membership could be issued for the LLC in this instance. Parents have class A membership with voting rights (regardless of percentage of ownership) and children have class B non-voting interest. If the amount of membership interest assigned each year does not exceed the $10,000 limit, no gift tax need be paid. The flexibility of the Operating Agreement of the LLC can be used to anticipate voluntary and involuntary transfers, and member death.

note An LLC has no limitations as to the number of members and no mandatory income distributions.

The LLC is a much more flexible vehicle than a trust that is typically used for this purpose. Parents can eliminate third party interests by restricting membership and determining the distributive rights of members.

There are many variations of this plan that can be used for any type real estate, family businesses, closely held businesses and some trusts. Seek out a qualified estate or financial planner who can tailor an LLC to your specific need in this area.

Creditor transactions

LLCs have distinct advantages when it comes to borrowing money from a creditor such as a bank. A creditor who seizes a member's interest in the LLC does not become a member of the company without the consent of the remaining members. Although the creditor only receives an assignment of membership interest, the amount of membership income allocated to his or her share must be reported for income tax purposes. If the LLC makes no actual distributions to that

> **note** Another important advantage LLCs have is the fact that company debts can be used to reduce the value of a member's investment in the LLC. This effectively reduces the tax basis of that member.

member, the creditor has actually incurred an expense and has received nothing in return. This may be a powerful deterrent to seizing membership interest.

Charitable organizations

It is possible to use an LLC in place of a limited partnership for the purpose of raising funds for charity. If the charitable donor is an LLC, the amount of deduction each partner can claim is proportional to each partner's equity in the LLC. For example, if a partner owns 15% of an LLC, on his or her own return, the partner may claim 15% of the company's donations.

Charitable organizations have traditionally participated in limited partnerships either as a sole partner or as one of several partners. However, this has caused complicated conflict-of-interest problems for the charities. By definition, they must be operated exclusively for the public interest and not for the benefit or interests of the limited partners.

There are two tests commonly used to determine charitable compliance:

1) the activity of the limited partnership must be such that it furthers the tax-exempt purpose of the charity

2) the obligations of the charity as general partner must not conflict with its ability to carry on its tax-exempt functions

note

As general partner, the charity must balance furthering its tax-exempt purpose with that of preserving and protecting the interest of the limited partners. This can be quite difficult as the two are often in direct conflict. Additionally, as general partner, the charity does not enjoy limited liability.

When the charity participates in an LLC instead of a limited partnership, it enjoys limited liability and maintains control over the LLC's activities. Some experts have suggested that if the charity is not a manager of the LLC, it may report as dividend income from its investment in the LLC any unrelated business income. As a general partner however, this option is unavailable.

The limited liability partnership

10

Chapter 10

The limited liability partnership

What you'll find in this chapter:

- When to choose the LLP for your business
- LLPs and limited liability
- Taxes and your LLP
- Forming the limited liability partnership
- Converting your business to an LLP

Most doctors, lawyers, accountants or other professionals carry insurance against malpractice and other types of litigation, because claims against these professionals are a daily occurrence. But no professional today can rely solely upon insurance for protection. There are now many other opportunities for professionals to incur liability arising from their practice. The need for sound organizational protection for professionals clearly matches that of the commercial business owner or family with wealth preservation concerns.

DEFINITION

Enter the LLC's cousin, the *limited liability partnership* (LLP), often called a registered limited liability partnership (RLLP) or a professional limited liability partnership (PLLP). After the late 1980's when law and accounting firms were being sued and their partners held liable for actions they had no knowledge of or hand in, states began creating an entity that would offer more protection to professionals. Texas and Louisiana led the way, and the LLP was born.

Why form an LLP?

In a general partnership, all partners are liable for any and all claims against the partnership, and creditors can seek personal assets of each partner. In a limited partnership, only the partnership itself and the general partner are liable; all limited partners enjoy the personal protection that corporate members have. An LLP is a partnership that is similar to an LLC in that all the partners are protected from liability, however with one significant difference.

note If Dr. Smith is sued for malpractice, the patient can only seek damages from the LLP and from Dr. Smith, and not from any of the other doctors in the LLP.

In an LLP, a partner is still personally liable for any claims of wrongdoing against him or her (such as malpractice). The critical difference is that the other partners in the LLP are not personally liable for another partner's actions, even if the partnership itself is held liable. In a general or limited partnership, all of the doctors in the partnership would be vulnerable to the lawsuit, but with an LLP, when one partner is personally liable the others are protected.

You can see why an LLP is so appealing to professionals. If the limited partnership is concerned with the loss of company assets to company creditors, the professional is concerned a hundred times over. Practicing under a limited liability partnership can offer them significantly more protection.

Limited liability in the LLP

The LLP protects the assets of individual partners, just as a corporation or LLC protects the assets of its members. Moreover, LLP assets cannot be directly seized by the professional partner's personal creditors, except when the negligent partner was acting on behalf of the LLP.

Keep in mind, however, that while the LLP protects the professional partner from both debts incurred by the practice and claims resulting from the malpractice of any other partner, it does not protect the professional partner from personal claims resulting from his own malpractice.

The very nature of the protection itself presents a different sort of problem than arises with other organizations. If the manager of the LLP, under whom everyone works and who himself works under a partner, is not shielded from malpractice of a partner, who would ever agree to be manager or supervisor? Most LLPs solve this problem by requiring that members indemnify a manager of the LLP.

Definition:

Indemnify. This means to secure against loss or damage which may occur in the future; to insure.

The degree of indemnification must be clearly set forth in the partnership agreement. A flexible partnership agreement can require the LLP's assets first be depleted, and it can prohibit any contributions made directly to third parties. In addition, the Agreement may not require contributions in cases of fraud or inappropriate conduct.

A partner in an LLP will not have limited liability under the following circumstances:

- the partner committed an act for which he is liable.

- the partner directed or supervised another partner or LLP representative who committed an act of liability while under the partner's direction/supervision

note The LLP does not protect a partner who is responsible for any act of malpractice, malfeasance or negligence.

- the partner was directly involved in a specific activity that included or resulted in an act of liability committed by another partner or LLP representative

This product does not constitute the rendering of legal advice or services. This product is intended for informational use only and is not a substitute for legal advice. State laws vary, so consult an attorney on all legal matters. This product was not prepared by a person licensed to practice law in this state. **97**

- the partner had knowledge or written notice of an act of liability committed by another partner or LLP representative

note

Another advantage of the LLP is that a liable partner's personal creditors cannot easily liquidate the partner's interest in the LLP. It is difficult for a personal creditor to liquidate assets, because ownership interest in this type of partnership must usually be by professionals within that profession. Without ownership, creditors can then not force a sale even if they claim the interest. This makes the LLP an excellent option when professionals want to participate in the management of the practice while insulating their personal assets from the partnership liabilities.

note

Even if the partner's personal assets are vulnerable and the LLP held liable, it is difficult for a creditor to cause significant damage to the LLP when they can not claim ownership interest in the LLP.

To make things even better, most states have adopted the Revised Uniform Partnership Act. The Act extends the LLP shield to cover not only tort claims but contract claims as well, offering even more protection. It's no surprise, then, that more and more businesses are making the LLP the business entity of choice.

Tax and the LLP

Like its cousin the limited liability company, the LLP avoids the double taxation of a corporation while maintaining the limited liability of a partnership. Partners in an LLP enjoy the same pass-through tax-status as the LLC; there is no tax on the partnership, only on personal income. It is one more advantage of choosing the LLP for your professional partnership.

Forming your LLP

Creating your LLP is quite simple, and involves only a moderate amount of work. Every state has its own requirements regarding the filing process, so be sure to contact your Secretary of State. There are four basic steps to form an LLP:

1)   *Register your LLP*. This is virtually the same as filing a general or limited partnership. Contact the Secretary of State where you wish to register for their specific filing requirements. Every state will ask you for at least the following:

- the name of the partnership. The name must include the words "Registered Limited Liability Partnership," "Limited Liability Partnership," "L.L.P.," or "LLP" at the end. Some states are even more specific regarding the name of an LLP.

- the address of the principal office

- the name and address of the LLP's registered agent for service of process

- a brief statement of the nature of business of the LLP

- names and addresses of the partners

2)   *Pay the filing fee.* Every year thereafter, there will be an annual renewal fee, due either by your anniversary of LLP registration or by a date set by your state.

3)   *Proof of insurance.* Most states require that you submit proof of insurance for all partners in the LLP; some states require additional security.

4)   ***Proof of licensure.*** Most states also require proof that the governing body of your particular profession deems each partner duly licensed to practice that profession in your state.

Once you have registered with the state, you will receive a date-stamped copy of your filing as proof of registration. This date will be your anniversary date. After that, you're ready for business.

Converting to an LLP

You may convert any business entity to an LLP, be it a general or limited partnership, LLC or corporation. To convert your business to an LLP, it is simply a matter of filing the registration with your state. Be sure to consult with your accountant and/or tax attorney, however, as your company's assets may be affected by such a conversion.

When partners convert their interests to LLC interest, the holding period or basis of any of the partners' interest is not affected. In addition, for tax purposes, the partnership is not terminated. The LLC continues to use the partnership's employer identification number (EIN) and uses the same tax year.

note When partners convert their interests to LLC interest, there is no gain or loss to any of the partners.

Follow these steps when converting your general or limited partnership or LLC to an LLP:

1)   Review your existing partnership or operating agreement and make amendments to reflect any changes in liability that will take place, and to ensure there will be no change in tax status of the partnership.

2) Document the partners'/members' election to attain LLP status, and any related provisions.

3) File your LLP registration with the state, fulfilling any insurance and professional requirements.

4) Register your new LLP name in each county you wish to do business in. This is to make known the new "LLP" portion of your company's name.

Upon conversion to an LLP, all assets now become the property of the LLP. Likewise, any all debts and obligations of the partnership or LLC remain the responsibility of the LLP. Conversion to an LLP does not create a new entity, but rather the LLP is considered to be the same entity as the partnership before the conversion. Therefore, any civil or criminal action or suit continues as if there had been no conversion. As per the agreement to elect LLP status, all partners of the partnership continue as partners in the LLP.

note
Conversion from a corporation may be quite complicated, so consult your attorney, accountant or tax specialist.

Points to remember

Any corporation or LLC that wishes to do business in a state other than the state of original registration must file in the other state as a foreign corporation or LLC. The same goes for LLPs, and the process is virtually the same as filing your original LLP. Your Secretary of State will have the forms you need for foreign registration. Keep in mind, however, that with a foreign LLP all partners must qualify with the governing board of your particular profession in every state you wish to register in.

note

Remember, an LLP can help to minimize the risk of its partners, but nothing can completely eliminate that risk. And don't mistakenly think you no longer need malpractice insurance if you form an LLP. Be certain you understand all of your state's requirements when filing your registration. Also, carefully consider taxes, state regulations for your profession, and malpractice insurance when creating your LLP Agreement.

Converting your business to an LLC

11

Chapter 11

Converting your business to an LLC

It is not uncommon to see an established businessperson slap his/her forehead and exclaim, "If I had only known about LLCs before I started my company!" If that is you, be assured that almost any business entity can be converted to an LLC. And this is commonly done. Many LLCs originated as other business entities.

Should you convert to an LLC?

It's not too late to convert your existing sole proprietorship, partnership or corporation to an LLC. Before converting any existing business, there are important issues to consider. While the prospect of limited liability and pass-through taxation are basic to the attraction, any existing business must consider other consequences of conversion. Here are six important elements to consider:

1) Does your state allow the conversion?

2) Are tax consequences associated with the conversion?

3) What is the procedure for conversion if there are no enabling statutory provisions?

4) What type of registration and disclosure laws must the company face?

5) What specific corporate, partnership and LLC laws must be complied with?

6) Does conversion obey existing creditor agreements?

Converting a sole proprietorship

A sole proprietorship is the easiest type of business entity to convert to an LLC because:

- there is no pre-existing formal structure

- a sole proprietorship is not a regulated business entity

- few documents are filed, and no articles, bylaws or governing charters need be addressed

Theoretically, all that need be done is to form an LLC, transfer the business assets and liabilities, and begin doing business as an LLC. Remember, however, that in more than half the states an LLC requires at least two members. Therefore, the sole proprietor may have to take in, and be able to work with, another member. The other member must also contribute assets to the LLC in exchange for the membership interest. The other member may be another business entity and may be a passive member.

There would be no tax liabilities if you transfer assets in this type of conversion, providing the assets transferred exceed or equal the liabilities transferred. Once the transfers are made, the members proceed as with any start-up LLC. All appropriate federal and state registration and disclosure laws as well as particular state LLC laws must be complied with. Carefully examine the specific situation before attempting conversion.

⚠ **CAUTION** When adding a member to a sole proprietorship to convert to an LLC, in order to avoid the trap of centralized management the new member may not be absent or silent.

For example, one popular solution often used by small businessmen in this situation is to gift the membership interest. This easily can be given to a spouse or other relative. There is no gift tax when the value of the gift does not exceed $10,000. Once the transfers are made, the members proceed as with any start-up LLC. All appropriate federal and state registration and disclosure laws as well as particular state LLC laws must be complied with.

If the special pass-through tax status is not of prime concern to you, but limited liability, simplicity and the flexibility of multi-state operations is, then creating a single member LLC is feasible.

E-Z TIP A careful examination of the specific circumstances affecting conversion should be made before any attempt at conversion is made.

Converting a partnership

Usually both general and limited partnerships may be converted to LLCs without any tax consequences or extraordinary filings. This is accomplished by having the LLC members maintain the same percentage ownership they had in the partnership.

Five ways to convert from a partnership to an LLC are:

1) *Modification of the partnership agreement.* The partnership agreement is simply changed to an LLC Operating Agreement by filing the partnership's Articles of Conversion with the appropriate state authority. The partners then follow the usual procedures for organizing an LLC in the chosen state by:

 a) filing the Articles of Organization with the state

 b) transferring assets and liabilities to the LLC via a bill of sale

By using this method, a formal dissolution of the partnership is not required.

2) *Exchange of interests.* This method does require a dissolution of the partnership by:

 a) exchanging partnership interests for LLC membership interests

 b) formally dissolving the partnership and the LLC receiving its assets and liabilities

3) *Formal dissolution.* Dissolving the partnership involves:

 a) deducting liabilities from assets and distributing remaining assets to the partners

 b) the partners assigning those assets to the LLC in exchange for membership interest

 c) filing dissolution with the proper state agencies and your creditors

The LLC now has all of the former partnership assets less its liabilities.

4) *Asset contribution.* This method requires the creation of a "dummy" third party, or "straw man."

   a) The LLC takes the partnership assets from which the partnership liabilities are to be deducted.

   b) In exchange, the LLC transfers back to the partnership 99% of the interest in the LLC's capital, profits and losses.

   c) The remaining 1 percent is transferred to the "straw man." This allows the LLC to comply with the requirement that it have at least two members.

   d) The partnership is formally dissolved.

   e) The 99 percent interest is distributed to each member according to the member's proportional share.

   f) The "straw man" is liquidated and the remaining 1 percent is redistributed to the members of the LLC.

5) *Merger.* If allowed by state law and the partnership agreement, a partnership may merge with an LLC without incurring a taxable event. When such a merger occurs, the LLC is the surviving entity. This type of merger usually requires the unanimous consent of the partners. If the state lacks statutory merger provisions for partnerships, a dissolution of the partnership may result.

> *note*
>
> The main advantage of using statutory merger provisions is that assets do not need to be exchanged. Sales, use and transfer taxes can be avoided because this exchange occurs by operation of law.

Converting a corporation

There are a variety of ways to convert a corporation to an LLC. However, such conversions almost always result in some tax liability. This nature of the tax liability depends upon whether the corporation is a C (regular) or S corporation and whether the conversion involves liquidating the corporation.

1) *C corporation:*

a) Corporate assets are distributed to shareholders, who then exchange those assets for membership interest in the LLC. The IRS considers this a taxable event for both the corporation and the shareholders. The distribution of assets to shareholders is considered payment in exchange for stock. The receipt of stock is considered income for the corporation and the distribution is income for the shareholders. Hence, double taxation. If the fair market value of the stock at the time it is received is more than the corporation's investment in it, a taxable gain results. If the shareholders receive more than their investment, a taxable gain also occurs. The contribution of assets to the LLC by shareholders, however, is tax free.

> *note* If the value of the distribution and receipt of stock is less than fair market value, a loss results and there may be no tax liability.

b) The corporation merges with the LLC. Not all states allow this type of merger but when it is allowed and the two companies combine, the LLC is the surviving company. The corporation is said to have *dissolved by consolidation* and, like any corporate dissolution, becomes a taxable event.

DEFINITION

2) ***S corporation:*** The pass-through tax advantages of an S corporation may be maintained even when merging with an LLC, because whatever taxes are incurred are passed through to the shareholders.

The IRS designed one exception to this pass through rule: Any C or S corporation converting to an LLC must pay taxes associated with the sale of appreciated property taking place up to 10 years before the switch to LLC status.

Basic merger statutes

There are five basic requirements to complete a merger:

1) There must be an agreement to merge. This is a formal document signed by the two companies and must contain the terms and conditions of the merger.

2) A required number of members or shareholders of each separate entity must approve the merger. If requirements for approval are not spelled out in the Operating Agreement of the LLC, state default rules govern the vote.

> *note* An agreement to merge must also outline the method by which interests will be converted from one entity to the other.

3) A certificate of merger is filed by the LLC but signed by both entities.

4) In some states, persons who object to the merger may have "dissenter's rights," which would need to be addressed.

5) If the corporation or partnership seeking conversion is a foreign corporation organized under the laws of another state, it must be allowed to merge under the laws of that state.

Dissolving your LLC

Chapter 12

Dissolving your LLC

DEFINITION

There are two broad ways to dissolve any business entity—through voluntary or involuntary dissolution. *Voluntary dissolution* involves action taken by the LLC according to provisions established in its Operating Agreement. *Involuntary dissolution* occurs by operation of law. For example, a court may order dissolution for:

- non-payment of taxes

- failure to maintain a registered agent or registered office

- membership misconduct

- failure of the LLC to return a membership contribution to a member

- completely merging with another firm

- disqualifying business activities. For example, an LLC cannot become a banking, financial or insurance institution. If there is any question about the legality of a new business activity, consult with the IRS.

note If you can show the court (or the IRS) that the LLC inadvertently violated one of the rules, it may allow the LLC to correct the problem and keep its status. But you should never anticipate this.

Common methods of dissolution

The three most common ways an LLC is dissolved are:

1) **Expiration.** This occurs when the expiration date of the LLC as set forth in the Articles of Organization and the Operating Agreement has been reached. As stated earlier, the period of duration is typically 30 years from the date of formation. Sometimes, instead of a fixed date, expiration results from the occurrence of a specific event. This is known as a "contingent expiration" and must also be included in the initial filings of the LLC. Dissolution by expiration is necessary in order that the LLC avoid having continuity of life. Having continuity of life could jeopardize the tax status of the LLC.

note Even if a member's withdrawal is not legal, the effect of dissolution is the same. The member however, may be subject to legal action for the wrongful act.

2) **Dissociation.** This usually occurs in accordance with state law, when a member withdraws from the LLC. While it may be a voluntary withdrawal such as in retirement or bankruptcy, it may also be involuntary as when a member is expelled, dies or becomes incapacitated.

The trend in some states is to allow a member to voluntarily withdraw without triggering dissolution. This is allowed if prior notice is given (usually at least 30 days) and is allowed even if it conflicts with provisions in the Operating Agreement.

In the event dissociation of a member triggers dissolution, the LLC may continue to exist in one of two ways:

1) The Operating Agreement or Articles of Organization may so state that the LLC should continue to exist. This is called continuation by prior agreement. If your state allows this type agreement, it is the preferred method. It effectively prevents a member who may lack the voting power to do so, from destroying the LLC.

2) In the absence of such a provision, the remaining members may consent to continue the LLC. This usually requires a vote. Some states accept a unanimous vote of the membership while others only a majority vote. Regardless of what type of vote an individual state requires, find out what the current IRS ruling is on voting requirements, as it may differ.

3) ***Agreement.*** An LLC may dissolve upon the consent of its members. This typically must be in writing and require the unanimous vote of the members.

Usually, it is a simple matter to dissolve a LLC. However, without an agreement, the partners may not foresee the consequences of dissolution. For example, who owns the name? Was advance compensation given for any reason? To avoid problems, you should get an LLC agreement first, with each partner having a lawyer.

The winding up process

Once dissolution has been triggered, the LLC must begin the winding up process. The company does not immediately cease to exist because it must

Definition:

Winding up is the procedure that is followed upon dissolution of a partnership.

have time to settle its affairs, dispose of its assets, pay debts and distribute remaining assets to its members. The Operating Agreement should require a final accounting and require all unfinished business during the dissolution period be completed before the winding up is complete.

Once done, the membership is spared liability for lingering claims.

Each year, thousands of businesses are started. Over half fail within four years. Sixty-five percent don't last six years. It is important to have an Operating Agreement since it is the dissolution and winding up phase that may most affect you financially.

Agency

The most common issue arising during the winding up stage is the problem of agency, or the authority of the membership to legally bind the LLC. Does the membership have continuing power to do business on behalf of the LLC? Let common sense become the rule of law. Only exercise authority as is appropriate to this stage of the business—contracts must be fulfilled, assets sold, debts paid, receivables collected, etc. Do not allow members to exceed their actual authority.

Any time the LLC enters into a long-term contract a written provision for cancellation in the event of dissolution should be included. Otherwise, the LLC may be liable for full performance upon dissolution.

Filing documents

All states require that documents be filed with the secretary of state. Some states require they be filed upon dissolution, others after the winding up process is completed or both. Typical documents include:

- Articles of Dissolution, Termination or Cancellation

- Notice of intent to dissolve. A public notice may be served upon unknown creditors by publishing a notice of dissolution in the newspaper.

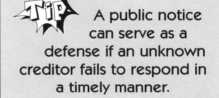

A public notice can serve as a defense if an unknown creditor fails to respond in a timely manner.

- Notice of winding up

- Advance notice to creditors. This document serves two purposes:

   1) It provides creditors with a cut off date by which claims for payment must be made. If the creditor does not respond within the allotted time, the LLC may be able to disregard the claim.

   2) It serves notice on third parties that the LLC is in dissolution and any further dealing with the company is done so as part of the winding up process.

Membership compensation

Persons involved in the winding up phase, be they members or managers, usually feel entitled to additional compensation for these activities. Any compensation due them should be clearly spelled out in the Operating Agreement. This will help avoid long drawn out battles as state law often does not address this issue directly.

Distribution of assets

Upon dissolution of the LLC, the claims of creditors must be satisfied first, before distributions are made to members. A creditor may be a third party or a member of the LLC. If the creditor is a member of the LLC, his or her claim must be a *non-equity claim*. This means the claim must exclude any right to distributions or return of capital.

Once creditors' claims are satisfied, a final distribution may be made to members. However, there is no standard rule by which members are paid. Who gets paid first is known as *priority*. The schedule of priority should be spelled out in the Operating Agreement, or if not, the LLC may rely upon the state statute. If you are relying upon the statute, find out what is required during the organizational stage of your LLC.

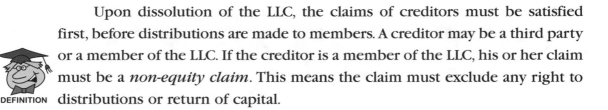

> *note* In most states, the procedure for dissolving an LLC follows the format for dissolving a corporation.

Some states require the capital contributed to the LLC be repaid before profits from distributions. Other states place priority of profits over capital. The Uniform Limited Partnership Act adopted by many states endorses the latter.

The forms in this guide

Operating Agreement

of

_____

adopted_____

LIMITED LIABILITY COMPANY OPERATING AGREEMENT
FOR_____

THIS LIMITED LIABILITY COMPANY OPERATING AGREEMENT (the Agreement) is made and entered into as of the _____ day of _____, _____ (year) by and among:

_____

_____

_____

and each individual or business entity as shall be subsequently admitted to the Company. These individuals and/or business entities shall be known as and referred to as "Members" and individually as a "Member." WHEREAS, the parties have formed a Limited Liability Company named above through their initial registered agent _____ pursuant to the laws of the State of _____. NOW, in consideration of the conditions and mutual covenants contained herein, and for good and valuable consideration, the parties agree upon the following terms and conditions:

ARTICLE I: COMPANY FORMATION

1. The members hereby form and organize the company as a Limited Liability Company subject to the provisions of the _____Limited Liability Company Act in effect as of this date. Articles of Organization shall be filed with the _____Secretary of State.

2. The members agree to execute this Operating Agreement and hereby acknowledge for good and valuable consideration receipt thereof. It is the intention of the members that this Operating Agreement shall be the sole source of agreement of the parties.

In the event any provision of this Operating Agreement is prohibited or rendered ineffective under the laws of_____, this Operating Agreement shall be considered amended to conform to the_____ Act as set forth in the Code of _____. The invalidity of any provision of this Operating Agreement shall not affect the subsequent validity of any other provisions of this Operating Agreement.

3. NAME. The name of the company shall be_____

_____. The business of the company shall be

conducted under that name or such trade or fictitious names as the members may determine.

4. DATE OF FORMATION. This Operating Agreement shall become effective upon its filing with

and acceptance by the appropriate state agency.

5. REGISTERED AGENT AND OFFICE. The company's initial registered agent and registered

office shall be _____

_____. Managing members may change the registered

agent or registered office at any time, by filing the necessary documents with the appropriate state

agency. Should managing members fail to act in this regard, any member may file such notice

of change in registered agent or registered office.

6. TERM. The company shall continue for a period of thirty (30) years from the date of formation

unless:

a)   The term is extended by amendment of the Operating Agreement. Members shall have

     the right to continue the business of the Company and may exercise that right by the

     unanimous vote of the remaining Members within ninety (90) days after the occurrence

     of the event described below.

b)   The company is dissolved by a majority vote of the membership.

c)   The death, resignation, expulsion, retirement, bankruptcy, incapacity or any other

     event that terminates the continued membership of a Member of the Company.

d)   Any event which makes it unlawful for the business of the Company to be carried

     on by the Members.

e)   Any other event causing the dissolution of a Limited Liability Company under the

     laws of the state of _____.

ARTICLE II: BUSINESS PURPOSE

It is the purpose of the Company to engage in_____

_____. The foregoing purposes and activities will be interpreted as examples only and not as limitations, and nothing therein shall be deemed as prohibiting the Company from extending its activities to any related or otherwise permissible lawful business purpose which may become necessary, profitable or desirable for the furtherance of the company objectives expressed above.

ARTICLE III: CAPITAL CONTRIBUTIONS

1. INITIAL CONTRIBUTIONS. Each Member shall contribute to the Company capital prior to or simultaneously with, the execution of this Agreement. Each Member shall have made initial capital contributions in the following amounts:

Name of Member	Value of Capital Contribution
_____	_____
_____	_____
_____	_____
_____	_____

No interest shall accrue on initial capital contributions.

2. ADDITIONAL CAPITAL CONTRIBUTIONS. If management decides that additional capital contributions are necessary for operating expenses or to meet other obligations, notice must be sent to each Member setting forth each Member's share of the total contribution. Such notice must be in writing and delivered to the Member at least ten (10) business days prior to the date the contribution is due. Any such additional capital contribution is strictly voluntary and any such commitment is to be considered a loan of capital by the Member to the Company. Such additional capital contribution does not in any way increase percentage of membership interest. This loan shall bear interest at _____ points above the current prime rate. Any loan under this subsection shall be paid in full before any distributions are made under Article IV.

3. THIRD PARTY BENEFICIARIES. Nothing in the foregoing sections is intended to benefit any creditor or third party to whom obligations are owed without the expressed written consent of the Company or any of its Members.

4. CAPITAL ACCOUNTS. A capital account shall be established by the Company for each Member. The capital account shall consist of:

   a) The amount of the Member's Capital Contributions to the Company including the fair market value of any property so contributed to the Company or distributed by the Company to the Member.

   b) Member's share of net profits or net losses and of any separate allocations of income, gain (including unrealized gain), loss or deduction. The maintenance of capital accounts shall at all times be in accordance with the requirements of state law.

5. ADDITIONAL PROVISIONS:

   a) Capital accounts shall be non-interest bearing accounts.

   b) Until the dissolution of the company, no Member may receive Company property in return for Capital contributions.

   c) The liability of any member for the losses or obligations incurred by the Company shall be limited to: Payment of capital contributions when due, *pro rata* share of undistributed Company assets and only to the extent required by law, any previous distributions to that Member from the Company.

ARTICLE IV: PROFITS, LOSSES ALLOCATIONS AND DISTRIBUTIONS

1. ALLOCATIONS. Net profits, losses, gains, deductions and credits from operations and financing shall be distributed among the Members in proportion to their respective interest and at such time as shall be determined by the Members.

2. DISTRIBUTIONS. Management may make distributions annually or more frequently if there is excess cash on hand after providing for appropriate expenses and liabilities. Such interim distributions are allocated to each Member according to percentage of membership interest.

ARTICLE V: MANAGEMENT

1. MANAGING MEMBERS. The names and addresses of Managing Members are:

_____

_____

_____

Managing Members shall make decisions regarding the usual affairs of the Company. A majority vote of the membership shall name as many managers as the Membership deem necessary and the membership shall elect one Chief Operating Manager who is responsible for carrying out the decisions of the managers.

2. NUMBER OF MANAGERS. The membership may elect one, but not fewer than one, manager.

3. TERM OF OFFICE. The term of office is not contractual but continues until:

   a) A fixed term of office, as designated by the membership, expires.

   b) The manager is removed with or without cause, by a majority vote of the membership.

   c) The dissociation of such manager.

4. AUTHORITY OF MANAGERS. Only managing members and authorized agents shall have the power to bind the Company. Each managing member is authorized on the Company's behalf to:

   a) Purchase, or otherwise acquire, sell, develop, pledge, convey, exchange, lease or otherwise dispose of Company assets wherever located.

   b) Initiate, prosecute and defend any proceeding on behalf of the Company.

   c) Incur and secure liabilities and obligations on behalf of the Company.

   d) Lend, invest or re-invest company assets as security for repayment. Money may be lent to members, employees and agents of the Company.

   e) Appoint officers and agents, and hire employees. It is also the province of management to define duties and establish levels of compensation. Management compensation will be determined by majority Membership vote.

   f) Execute and deliver all contracts, conveyances, assignments, leases, subleases, franchise and licensing agreements, promissory notes, loans, security agreements or any other kind relating to Company business.

g) Establish pensions, trusts, life insurance, incentive plans or any variation thereof, for the benefit of any or all current or former employees, members and agents of the Company.

h) Make charitable donations in the Company's name.

i) Seek advice from members not part of elected management, although, such advice need not be heeded.

j) Supply, upon the request of any Member, information about the Company or any of its activities including but not limited to, access to company records for the purpose of inspecting and copying company books, records and materials in the possession of management. The Requesting Member shall be responsible for any expenses incurred in the exercise of these rights set forth in this document.

5. STANDARD OF CARE AND EXCULPATION. Any member of management must refrain from engaging in grossly negligent, reckless or intentional misconduct. Any act or omission of a member of management that results in loss or damage to the company or Member, if done in good faith, shall not make the manager liable to the Members.

6. INDEMNIFICATION. The Company shall indemnify its Members, Managers, employees and agents as follows:

a) Every Manager, agent, or employee of the Company shall be indemnified by the Company against all expenses and liabilities, including counsel fees reasonably incurred by him in connection with any proceeding to which he may become involved, by reason of his being or having been a Member of the Company or having served at the request of the Company as a Manager, employee, or agent of the Company or any settlement thereof, whether or not he is a manager, employee or agent at the time such expenses are incurred, except in such cases wherein the Manager, agent or employee is adjudged guilty of willful misfeasance or malfeasance in the performance of his duties; provided that in the event of a settlement the indemnification herein shall apply only when the Managers approve such settlement and reimbursement as being for the best interests of the Company.

b) The Company shall provide to any person who is or was a Member, Manager, employee, or agent of the Company or is or was serving at the request of the Company as Manager, employee, or agent of the Company, the indemnity against expenses of suit, litigation or other proceedings which is specifically permissible under applicable law.

ARTICLE VI: TAX AND ACCOUNTING MATTERS

1. BANK ACCOUNTS. Management shall establish bank accounts, deposit company funds in those accounts and make disbursements from those accounts.

2. ACCOUNTING METHOD. The cash method of accounting shall be the accounting method used to keep records of receipts and disbursements.

3. TMP. A Tax Matter Partner shall be designated by the management of the company as designated by the IRS Code.

4. YEARS. The fiscal and tax years of the Company shall be chosen by management.

5. ACCOUNTANT. An independent accountant shall be selected by management.

ARTICLE VII: MEMBER DISSOCIATION

1. Upon the first occurrence of any of the following events, a person shall cease to be a member of the Company:

a) The bankruptcy of the member.

b) The death or court-ordered adjudication of incapacity of the member.

c) The withdrawal of a member with the consent of a majority vote of the remaining membership.

d) The dissolution and winding up of the non-corporate business member including the termination of a trust.

e) The filing of a Certificate of Dissolution by the corporate member.

f) The complete liquidation of an estate's interest in the LLC.

g) The expulsion of the member with the majority consent of the remaining membership.

h) The expiration of the term specified in Article I, section 6.

2. OPTION TO PURCHASE INTEREST. In the event of dissociation of a Member, the Company shall have the right to purchase the former Member's interest at current fair market value.

ARTICLE VIII: DISPOSITION OF MEMBERSHIP INTERESTS

1. PROHIBITIONS.

   a) No membership interest, be it a sale, assignment, exchange, transfer, mortgage, pledge or grant, shall be disposed of if the disposition would result in the dissolution of the Company without full compliance with all appropriate state and federal laws.

   b) No member may in any way alienate all or part of his membership interest in the Company be it through assignment, conveyance, encumbrance or sale, without the prior written consent of the majority of the remaining members. Such consent may be given, withheld or delayed as the remaining members see fit.

2. PERMISSIONS. A Member may assign his membership interest in the Company subject to the provisions in this article. The assignment of membership interest does not in itself entitle the assignee to participate in the management of the Company nor is the assignee entitled to become a member of the Company. The assignee is not a substitute member but only an assignee of membership interest and as such, is entitled to receive the income and distributions the assigning member would have otherwise received.

3. SUBSTITUTE MEMBERSHIP. Only upon the unanimous consent of the remaining members may an assignee of membership interest become a substitute member and be entitled to all rights associated with the assignor. Upon such admission, the substitute member is subject to all restrictions and liabilities of a Member.

ARTICLE IX: MEETINGS

1. VOTING. All members shall have the right to vote on all of the following:

   a) The dissolution of the Company.

   b) The merger of the Company.

   c) Any transaction involving any potential conflict of interest.

d) An amendment to the Articles of Organization or to the Operating Agreement.

e) The transfer or disposition of all Company assets outside the ordinary course of business.

2. REQUIRED VOTE. Unless a greater vote is required by statute or the Articles of Organization, an affirmative vote of the majority of the membership shall be required.

3. MEETINGS.

    a) The manager(s) shall hold an annual meeting at a time and place of their choosing.

    b) Special meetings of the membership may be called at any time by the manager(s) or by at least ten (10%) of the membership interest of all members. Written notice of such meeting must be provided at least sixty (60) business days prior and not later than ten (10) days before the date of the meeting. A member may elect to participate in any meeting via telephone.

4. CONSENT. In the absence of an annual or special meeting and in the absence of a vote, any action required to be taken may be permitted with the written consent of the members having not less than the minimum number of votes required to authorize such action at a meeting.

ARTICLE X: DISSOLUTION AND TERMINATION

In the event a dissolution event occurs the remaining membership shall have the option to elect to continue the company as defined by Article I, section 6.

1. MERGER. In the event the election to continue the company following a dissolution event is not obtained, a majority vote of the remaining members may elect to reconstitute the Company through merger with and into another Limited Liability Company pursuant to applicable state law.

2. WINDING UP. If the members do not elect to continue the Company or reconstitute it, the Manager or other person selected by a majority vote of the membership shall wind up the Company.

3. FINAL DISTRIBUTIONS. After all Company assets have been liquidated and all Company debts have been paid, the proceeds of such liquidation shall be distributed to members in accordance

with their capital account balance. Liquidation proceeds shall be paid within _____ days of the end of the Company's taxable year or, if later, within _____ days after the date of liquidation.

4. DISSOLUTION. Upon completion of the winding up period, the Manager or other person selected shall file with the Secretary of State the Certificate of Dissolution or its equivalent and any other appropriate documents as required by law.

IN WITNESS WHEREOF, the parties hereto make and execute this Operating Agreement on the dates set below their names, to be effective on the date first above written.

Signed and Agreed this _____ day of _____ , _____(year).

By

Manager: _____

Member: _____

Member: _____

Member: _____

CERTIFICATE OF AMENDMENT

_____

, a limited liability company of the

State of   whose registered office is located at

, certifies pursuant to the provisions of

, that at a meeting of the shareholders of said

limited liability company called for the purpose of amending the Articles of Organization, and

held on   ,   (year), it was resolved by the vote of the holders of an

appropriate majority of the shares of each class entitled to vote that ARTICLE of the Articles of

Organization is amended to read as follows:

ARTICLE

Signed on_____, _____(year)

By_____
Manager

_____
Secretary

MINUTES OF _____ MEETING

_____

A regular meeting of the Managers of   was

held at   on   ,   , at

.m.

The following were present and participated at the meeting:

_____

_____

_____

being all the Managers of the Company.

                    , Manager of the Company, acted as Chairman of the meeting, and

                    , Secretary of the Company, acted as Secretary of the

meeting.

The Secretary put forth a waiver of notice of the meeting, signed by all the Managers, and
accordingly filed the waiver of notice with the minutes of the meeting.

The Chairman stated that a quorum of the Managers was present, and that the meeting,
having been duly convened, could transact business.

The minutes of the regular meeting of the Managers held on   ,
(year), were read and approved.

On the motion duly made and seconded, and after due deliberation, the following resolution was made:

A vote was taken which showed:

In Favor of Motion

_____, representing   shares

_____, representing   shares

_____, representing   shares

Opposed to Motion

_____, representing   shares

_____, representing   shares

Not Voting on Motion

_____, representing   shares

    The Secretary announced that   shares had been voted in favor of the said resolution and   shares had been voted against said resolution, said vote representing more than   percent of outstanding shares in attendance and entitled to vote thereon.

    The Managers thereafter declared that the resolution had been duly adopted.

    There being no further business, upon motion duly made, the meeting adjourned.

_____
Secretary

_____
Date

Name & Address of Member	Title Director Member Manager Assignee	Dates of Membership From - To	Capital Contributions (cash, property, etc.)

LIMITED LIABILITY COMPANY REGISTER, cont.

Name & Address of Member	Title Director Member Manager Assignee	Dates of Membership From - To	Capital Contributions (cash, property, etc.)

BILL OF SALE

FOR VALUE RECEIVED, the undersigned

of   hereby sells and transfers unto

of   (Buyer),

and its successors and assigns forever, the following described goods and chattels:

Seller warrants and represents that it has good title to said property, full authority to sell and transfer same and that said goods and chattels are being sold free and clear of all liens, encumbrances, liabilities and adverse claims, of every nature and description.

Seller further warrants that it shall fully defend, protect, indemnify and save harmless the Buyer and its lawful successors and assigns from any and all adverse claim, that may be made by any party against said goods.

It is provided, however, that Seller disclaims any implied warranty of condition, merchantability or fitness for a particular purpose. Said goods being sold in their present condition "as is" and "where is."

Signed this   day of   ,   (year).

In the presence of:

_____   _____
Witness' Signature   Seller's Signature

_____   _____
Print Name of Witness   Address of Seller

_____   _____
Address of Witness   Buyer's Signature

                                                     _____
                                                     Address of Buyer

QUITCLAIM DEED

THIS QUITCLAIM DEED, Executed this   day of   ,   (year),

by first party, Grantor,

whose post office address is

to second party, Grantee,

whose post office address is

WITNESSETH, That the said first party, for good consideration and for the sum of
                              Dollars ($) paid by the said second
party, the receipt whereof is hereby acknowledged, does hereby remise, release and quitclaim
unto the said second party forever, all the right, title, interest and claim which the said first party
has in and to the following described parcel of land, and improvements and appurtenances there-
to in the County of   , State of   to wit:

IN WITNESS WHEREOF, The said first party has signed and sealed these presents the day and year first above written. Signed, sealed and delivered in presence of:

_____

Signature of Witness

_____

Print name of Witness

_____

Signature of Witness

_____

Print name of Witness

_____

Signature of First Party

_____

Print name of First Party

_____

Signature of First Party

_____

Print name of First Party

State of _____ }
County of _____
On _____ before me, _____,
appeared _____
personally known to me (or proved to me on the basis of satisfactory evidence) to be the person(s) whose name(s) is/are subscribed to the within instrument and acknowledged to me that he/she/they executed the same in his/her/their authorized capacity(ies), and that by his/her/their signature(s) on the instrument the person(s), or the entity upon behalf of which the person(s) acted, executed the instrument.
WITNESS my hand and official seal.

_____

Signature of Notary

Affiant _____Known_____Produced ID

Type of ID _____

(Seal)

State of _____ }
County of _____
On _____ before me, _____,
appeared _____
personally known to me (or proved to me on the basis of satisfactory evidence) to be the person(s) whose name(s) is/are subscribed to the within instrument and acknowledged to me that he/she/they executed the same in his/her/their authorized capacity(ies), and that by his/her/their signature(s) on the instrument the person(s), or the entity upon behalf of which the person(s) acted, executed the instrument.
WITNESS my hand and official seal.

_____

Signature of Notary

Affiant _____Known_____Produced ID

Type of ID _____

(Seal)

_____

Signature of Preparer

_____

Print Name of Preparer

_____

Address of Preparer

ASSIGNMENT OF ASSETS

TO

_____

BE IT KNOWN, for value received, the undersigned   of

                        hereby unconditionally and irrevocably assigns and trans-

fers unto   of   all right, title and

interest in and to the following:

The undersigned fully warrants that it has full rights and authority to enter into this assign-

ment and that the rights and benefits assigned hereunder are free and clear of any lien, encum-

brance, adverse claim or interest by any third party.

This assignment shall be binding upon and inure to the benefit of the parties, and their suc-

cessors and assigns.

Signed this   day of   ,   (year).

_____   _____
Witness' Signature   Assignor's Signature

_____   _____
Print Name of Witness   Print Name of Assignor

_____   _____
Address of Witness   Address of Assignor

_____   _____
Witness' Signature   Assignee's Signature

_____   _____
Print Name of Witness   Print Name of Assignee

_____   _____
Address of Witness   Address of Assignee

Glossary of useful terms

A-C

Articles of Organization

A document filed with the Secretary of State that creates a limited liability company. It can include the name of the company, its purpose, the principal address of business, the Registered Agent's name and address, duration of the company, and its members.

Assets

Anything owned with monetary value. This includes both real and personal property.

Asset protection

A form of financial self-defense which places assets beyond the reach of creditors.

Bulletproof statutes

State statutes governing LLC formation that, if followed, assure the LLC it will be taxed as a partnership for federal tax purposes.

C Corporation

Any corporation that is not an S corporation.

Calendar year

The accounting year beginning January 1 and ending on December 31.

C-F

Certificate of Organization

The document that creates an LLC according to the laws of the state. This must be filed and approved by the state.

Corporation

A business formed and authorized by law to act as a single entity, although it may be owned by one or more persons. It is legally endowed with rights and responsibilities and has a life of its own independent of the owners and operators. The owners are not personally liable for debts or obligations of the corporation.

Default rules

Statutory rules that take effect in the absence of contrary provisions in an Operating Agreement.

Dissolution

Formal statutory liquidation, termination and winding up of a business entity.

Distribution

Payment of cash or property to a member, shareholder or partner according to his or her percentage of ownership.

Double taxation

Occurs when corporations pay tax on corporate profits and shareholders pay income tax on dividend or distributive income.

Fictitious business name

A name other than the registered name under which a company may do business as long as it is not used for fraudulent purposes.

F-I

Fiscal year

Any 12-month period used by a business as its fiscal accounting period. Such accounting period may, for example, run from July 1 of one year through June 30 of the next year.

Flexible statutes

State formation statutes that allow an LLC options that exceed IRS guidelines for special tax status.

Foreign LLC

A limited liability company formed in one state or coun- try but conducting some or all of its business in another state or country.

Free transfer of interests

The ability to transfer a membership interest to a non-member without consent of the other members.

General partner

The partner who accepts personal liability and is responsible for the daily management of a partnership.

Gift

For tax purposes, the IRS recognizes as a gift any voluntary transfer of property without consideration whose value does not exceed $10,000.

Incorporate

To form a corporation or to organize and be granted status as a corporation by following procedures prescribed by law.

I-M

Indemnification

Financial or other protection provided by an LLC or corporation to its members, managers, directors, officers and employees, which protects them against expenses and liabilities in lawsuits alleging they breached some duty in their service to, or on behalf of, the company.

Insolvency

Being unable to pay one's debts because liabilities exceed assets.

Limited liability

The condition in LLCs and corporations that frees owners from being personally liable for debts and obligations of the company, with a few tax-related exceptions. With company or corporate debt, general creditors cannot attach the owners' homes, cars and other personal property.

Limited liability company

A business entity created by legislation that offers its owners the limited personal liability of a corporation and the tax advantages of a partnership.

Limited partner

A partner who contributes capital or property to the partnership and enjoys limited liability to the extent of his or her investment but who may not participate in the management of the partnership.

Member

One who contributes capital, property or services to an LLC and in return, receives a membership interest in the company.

Membership interest

The right to vote, participate in management decisions and receive distributions from the company.

Merger

The absorption of one company by another.

O-S

Operating Agreement

A statement of the general principles of a limited liability company which combines information from the Articles of Organization with resolutions passed unanimously by members. It details economic and management arrangements as well as members' rights and responsibilities.

Pass-through tax status

Profits that are not taxed on the company level but are distributed directly to members who report such profits as dividend income.

Pro rata

Members receive rights or dividends based upon percentage of ownership.

Sole proprietorship

A business owned by an individual who is solely responsible for all aspects of the business, and where the business and its owners are thus considered the same entity.

State statutes

Laws created by a state legislature.

Statutory agent

A lawyer, corporation or individual who has assumed the responsibility of being the legal representative for a company for purposes of accepting legal documents (including service) in a certain state.

S Corporation (Subchapter S Corporation)

A small business corporation which elects to be taxed as a partnership or proprietorship for federal income tax purposes. Individual shareholders enjoy the benefits under state law of limited corporate liability, but avoid corporate federal taxes.

Resources

••• Online •••

◆ **American Academy of Estate Planning Attorneys**

URL: http://www.aaepa.com

◆ **American Express Small Business Exchange**

URL: http://www.americanexpress.com/smallbusiness

◆ **BizProWeb**

URL: http://www.bizproweb.com

◆ **Entrepreneur's Help Page**

URL: http://www.tannedfeet.com

◆ **MSN Money Central**

URL: http://moneycentral.msn.com/articles/tax/basics/

2822.asp

◆ **National Federation of Independent Business**

URL: http://www.nfibonline.com

◆ **Small Business Administration**

URL: http://www.sbaonline.sba.gov

◆ **Small Business Advisor**

URL: http://www.isquare.com

◆ **U.S. Business Advisor**

URL: http://www.business.gov

◆ **U.S. Small Business Administration**

URL: http://www.sbaonline.sba.gov/starting

••• Related Links •••

◆ **Council of Better Business Bureaus, Inc.**

URL: http://www.bbb.org

◆ **Education Index, Business Resources**

URL: http://www.educationindex.com/bus

◆ **Estate Planning Links**

URL: http://users.aol.com/dmk58/epl.html

◆ **Inc. Online**

http://www.inc.com

◆ **Internet Law Library**

URL: http://law.house.gov/329.htm

◆ **National Center for Employee Ownership**

URL: http://www.nceo.org/index.html

◆ **National SBDC Research Network**

URL: http://www.smallbiz.suny.edu

◆ **Small Business Primer**

URL: http://www.ces.ncsu.edu/depts/fcs/business/welcome.html

···Legal Search Engines···

◆ **All Law**

  http://www.alllaw.com

◆ **American Law Sources On Line**

  http://www.lawsource.com/also/searchfm.htm

◆ **Catalaw**

  http://www.catalaw.com

◆ **FindLaw**

  URL: http://www.findlaw.com

◆ **Hieros Gamos**

  http://www.hg.org/hg.html

◆ **InternetOracle**

  http://www.internetoracle.com/legal.htm

◆ **LawAid**

  http://www.lawaid.com/search.html

◆ **LawCrawler**

  http://www.lawcrawler.com

◆ **LawEngine, The**

  http://www.fastsearch.com/law

◆ **LawRunner**

http://www.lawrunner.com

◆ **'Lectric Law Library**™

URL: http://www.lectlaw.com

◆ **Legal Search Engines**

http://www.dreamscape.com/frankvad/search.legal.html

◆ **LEXIS/NEXIS Communications Center**

http://www.lexis-nexis.com/lncc/general/search.html

◆ **Meta-Index for U.S. Legal Research**

http://gsulaw.gsu.edu/metaindex

◆ **Seamless Website, The**

http://seamless.com

◆ **USALaw**

http://www.usalaw.com/linksrch.cfm

◆ **WestLaw**

http://westdoc.com

Registered users only. Fee paid service.

••• State Bar Associations •••

ALABAMA

Alabama State Bar
415 Dexter Avenue
Montgomery, AL 36104

mailing address:
PO Box 671
Montgomery, AL 36101
(205) 269-1515

http://www.alabar.org/

ALASKA

Alaska Bar Association
510 L Street No. 602
Anchorage, AK 99501

mailing address
PO Box 100279
Anchorage, AK 99510

ARIZONA

State Bar of Arizona
111 West Monroe
Phoenix, AZ 85003-1742
(602) 252-4804

ARKANSAS

Arkansas Bar Association
400 West Markham
Little Rock, AR 72201
(501) 375-4605

CALIFORNIA

State Bar of California
555 Franklin Street
San Francisco, CA 94102
(415) 561-8200

http://www.calbar.org/
Alameda County Bar
Association

http://www.acbanet.org/

COLORADO

Colorado Bar Association
No. 950, 1900 Grant Street
Denver, CO 80203
(303) 860-1115

*http://www.usa.net/cobar/
index.htm*

CONNECTICUT

Connecticut Bar Association
101 Corporate Place
Rocky Hill, CT 06067-1894
(203) 721-0025

DELAWARE

Delaware State Bar Association
1225 King Street, 10th floor
Wilmington, DE 19801
(302) 658-5279
(302) 658-5278 (lawyer referral
service)

DISTRICT OF COLUMBIA

District of Columbia Bar
1250 H Street, NW, 6th Floor
Washington, DC 20005
(202) 737-4700

Bar Association of the District
of Columbia
1819 H Street, NW, 12th floor
Washington, DC 20006-3690
(202) 223-6600

FLORIDA

The Florida Bar
The Florida Bar Center
650 Apalachee Parkway
Tallahassee, FL 32399-2300
(904) 561-5600

GEORGIA

State Bar of Georgia
800 The Hurt Building
50 Hurt Plaza
Atlanta, GA 30303
(404) 527-8700

http://www.kuesterlaw.com/
comp.html

HAWAII

Hawaii State Bar Association
1136 Union Mall
Penthouse 1
Honolulu, HI 96813
(808) 537-1868

http://www.hsba.org/

IDAHO

Idaho State Bar
PO Box 895
Boise, ID 83701
(208) 334-4500

ILLINOIS

Illinois State Bar Association
424 South Second Street
Springfield, IL 62701
(217) 525-1760

INDIANA

Indiana State Bar Association
230 East Ohio Street
Indianapolis, IN 46204
(317) 639-5465

http://www.iquest.net/isba/

IOWA

Iowa State Bar Association
521 East Locust
Des Moines, IA 50309
(515) 243-3179

http://www.iowabar.org

KANSAS

Kansas Bar Association
1200 Harrison Street
Topeka, KS 66601
(913) 234-5696

http://www.ink.org/public/
cybar/

KENTUCKY

Kentucky Bar Association
514 West Main Street
Frankfort, KY 40601-1883
(502) 564-3795

http://www.kybar.org/

LOUISIANA

Louisiana State Bar Association
601 St. Charles Avenue
New Orleans, LA 70130
(504) 566-1600

MAINE

Maine State Bar Association
124 State Street
PO Box 788
Augusta, ME 04330
(207) 622-7523

http://www.mainebar.org/

MARYLAND

Maryland State Bar Association
520 West Fayette Street
Baltimore, MD 21201
(410) 685-7878

http://www.msba.org/msba/

MASSACHUSETTS

Massachusetts Bar Association
20 West Street
Boston, MA 02111
(617) 542-3602
(617) 542-9103 (lawyer referral service)

MICHIGAN

State Bar of Michigan
306 Townsend Street
Lansing, MI 48933-2083
(517) 372-9030

http://www.umich.edu/~icle

MINNESOTA

Minnesota State Bar Association
514 Nicollet Mall
Minneapolis, MN 55402
(612) 333-1183

MISSISSIPPI

The Mississippi Bar
643 No. State Street
Jackson, Mississippi 39202
(601) 948-4471

MISSOURI

The Missouri Bar
P.O. Box 119, 326 Monroe
Jefferson City, Missouri 65102
(314) 635-4128

http://www.mobar.org

MONTANA

State Bar of Montana
46 North Main
PO Box 577
Helena, MT 59624
(406) 442-7660

NEBRASKA

Nebraska State Bar Association
635 South 14th Street, 2nd floor
Lincoln, NE 68508
(402) 475-7091

http://www.nol.org/legal/
nsba/index.html

NEVADA

State Bar of Nevada
201 Las Vegas Blvd.
Las Vegas, NV 89101
(702) 382-2200

http://www.dsi.org/statebar
/nevada.htm

NEW HAMPSHIRE

New Hampshire Bar
Association
112 Pleasant Street
Concord, NH 03301
(603) 224-6942

NEW JERSEY

New Jersey State Bar
Association
One Constitution Square
New Brunswuck, NJ 08901-1500
(908) 249-5000

NEW MEXICO

State Bar of New Mexico
121 Tijeras Street N.E.
Albuquerque, NM 87102

mailing address:
PO Box 25883
Albuquerque, NM 87125
(505) 843-6132

NEW YORK

New York State Bar Association
One Elk Street
Albany, NY 12207
(518) 463-3200

http://www.nysba.org/

NORTH CAROLINA

North Carolina State Bar
208 Fayetteville Street Mall
Raleigh, NC 27601

mailing address:
PO Box 25908
Raleigh, NC 27611
(919) 828-4620

North Carolina Bar Association
1312 Annapolis Drive
Raleigh, NC 27608

mailing address:
PO Box 12806
Raleigh, NC 27605
(919) 828-0561

http://www.barlinc.org/

NORTH DAKOTA

State Bar Association of North
Dakota
515 1/2 East Broadway, suite 101
Bismarck, ND 58501

mailing address:
PO Box 2136
Bismarck, ND 58502
(701) 255-1404

OHIO

Ohio State Bar Association
1700 Lake Shore Drive
Columbus, OH 43204

mailing address:
PO Box 16562
Columbus, OH 43216-6562
(614) 487-2050

OKLAHOMA

Oklahoma Bar Association
1901 North Lincoln
Oklahoma City, OK 73105
(405) 524-2365

OREGON

Oregon State Bar
5200 S.W. Meadows Road
PO Box 1689
Lake Oswego, OR 97035-0889
(503) 620-0222

PENNSYLVANIA

Pennsylvannia Bar Association
100 South Street
PO Box 186
Harrisburg, PA 17108
(717) 238-6715

Pennsylvania Bar Institute

http://www.pbi.org

PUERTO RICO

Puerto Rico Bar Association
PO Box 1900
San Juan, Puerto Rico 00903
(809) 721-3358

RHODE ISLAND

Rhode Island Bar Association
115 Cedar Street
Providence, RI 02903
(401) 421-5740

SOUTH CAROLINA

South Carolina Bar
950 Taylor Street
PO Box 608
Columbia, SC 29202
(803) 799-6653

http://www.scbar.org/

SOUTH DAKOTA

State Bar of South Dakota
222 East Capitol
Pierre, SD 57501
(605) 224-7554

TENNESSEE

Tennessee Bar Assn
3622 West End Avenue
Nashville, TN 37205
(615) 383-7421

http://www.tba.org/

TEXAS

State Bar of Texas
1414 Colorado
PO Box 12487
Austin, TX 78711
(512) 463-1463

UTAH

Utah State Bar
645 South 200 East, Suite 310
Salt Lake City, UT 84111
(801) 531-9077

VERMONT

Vermont Bar Association
PO Box 100
Montpelier, VT 05601
(802) 223-2020

VIRGINIA

Virginia State Bar
707 East Main Street, suite 1500
Richmond, VA 23219-0501
(804) 775-0500

Virginia Bar Association
701 East Franklin St., Suite 1120
Richmond, VA 23219
(804) 644-0041

VIRGIN ISLANDS

Virgin Islands Bar Association
P.O. Box 4108
Christiansted, Virgin Islands
00822
(809) 778-7497

WASHINGTON

Washington State Bar
Association
500 Westin Street
2001 Sixth Avenue
Seattle, WA 98121-2599
(206) 727-8200

http://www.wsba.org/

WEST VIRGINIA

West Virginia State Bar
2006 Kanawha Blvd. East
Charleston, WV 25311
(304) 558-2456

http://www.wvbar.org

West Virginia Bar Association
904 Security Building
100 Capitol Street
Charleston, WV 25301
(304) 342-1474

WISCONSIN

State Bar of Wisconsin
402 West Wilson Street
Madison, WI 53703
(608) 257-3838

http://www.wisbar.org/
home.htm

WYOMING

Wyoming State Bar
500 Randall Avenue
Cheyenne, WY 82001
PO Box 109
Cheyenne, WY 82003
(307) 632-9061

APPENDIX:

LLC REGISTRATION

AND OPERATION REQUIREMENTS

and

DEPARTMENTS OF LLC REGISTRATION

BY STATE

The following requirements are subject to change.
Contact your appropriate state office for updated information.

ALABAMA

Date of law	Status	Filing Fees	State Statute	Minimum Membership
October 1, 1993	Flexible	$45	The Alabama LLC Act ALA. CODE s.10-12-1 through 10-12-61	At least two members

Foreign LLCs	Domestic LLCs	State Entity Tax	State Tax Classification	IRS Revenue Ruling
Recognized	Recognized	None	Alabama follows federal income tax classifications	94-6

Required Records	Correspondence
• Names and addresses of all managers and members • Articles of Organization and amendments • All financial statements for three years • All federal, state, and local tax returns for three years • Current Operating Agreement	Secretary of State State Capitol Corporations Div. P.O. Box 5616 Montgomery, AL 36103-5616 (334) 242-5324

Default Rules for LLC Operation	Requirements for Articles of Organization
• The LLC is member managed • Any member can withdraw from the LLC upon 30 days notice • Membership interest is not assignable; it is an act of dissociation • The LLC does not dissolve upon assignment • Assignee's interest is financial only • Assignor retains membership interest • Unanimous vote of remaining membership required to admit assignee • Assignment does not release assignor from obligations to the LLC • Profits and losses distributed on *pro rata* basis	• Articles of Organization must include the name "Limited Liability Company" or the initials "L.L.C." • Duration (if less than perpetual) • Purpose of the company • Name of Registered Agent in Alabama • Address of Registered Office • Names and addresses of initial membership • Conditions for admitting new members • Right to continue following dissolution or act of dissociation • Whether the company will be manager or member managed

ALASKA

Date of law	Status	Filing Fees	State Statute	Minimum Membership
July 1, 1995	Flexible	$250	The Alaska LLC Act ALASKA STATUTE s. 1.50.010 through 10.50.990	At least two members

Foreign LLCs	Domestic LLCs	State Entity Tax	State Tax Classification	IRS Revenue Ruling
Recognized	Recognized	None	Alaska follows federal income tax classifications	None

Required Records	Correspondence
• Names and addresses of all managers and members • Articles of Organization and all amendments • All federal, state, and local tax returns for three years • Operating Agreement and all amendments	State of Alaska Department of Commerce and Economic Development Div. of Banking, Securities & Corporations Juneau, AL 99811-0807 (907) 465-2521

Default Rules for LLC Operation	Requirements for Articles of Organization
• The LLC must be member managed • Any member, upon providing 30 days written notice, can withdraw from the LLC at any time • Company actions require the unanimous vote of the membership • Although membership interest may be assigned without restriction, the assignee has no right to participate in the management of the company	• Articles of Organization must include the name "Limited Liability Company" or the initials "L.L.C" or "LLC". The words "city" or "borough" may not appear in the name. • Duration (if less than perpetual) • Purpose of the company • Name and address of Registered Agent in Alaska • Address of Registered Office • Original and one copy of the Articles filed with Secretary of State on 8 1/2" x 11" paper • Statement that the Articles are being filed under Alaska Limited Liability Act • Description of the business according to the Standard Industrial Classification codes • Articles signed by either the members or the managers • Whether the company will be manager or member managed

ARIZONA

Date of law	Status	Filing Fees	State Statute	Minimum Membership
September 30, 1992	Flexible	$50 filing fee $150 publ. fee $10 name reserv.	ARIZ REV. STAT. ANN. s. 29-601 through s. 29-857	At least two members

Foreign LLCs	Domestic LLCs	State Entity Tax	State Tax Classification	IRS Revenue Ruling
Recognized	Recognized	None	Arizona follows federal income tax classifications	93-93

Required Records	Correspondence
• Names and addresses of all managers and members • Articles of Organization and amendments • All financial statements for three years • All federal, state, and local tax returns for three years • Current Operating Agreement	Arizona Corporation Commission Incorporating Division 1300 W. Washington St., 3rd Floor Phoenix, AZ 85007 (602) 542-4786

Default Rules for LLC Operation	Requirements for Articles of Organization
• The LLC is member managed • Profits and losses will be distributed or apportioned to members on a *pro rata* basis • Company decisions, authorized distributions, repurchase of a member's interest and filing winding up notices require the majority vote of the membership • Activities beyond the scope of the company's stated business purpose, merger or consolidation plans, issuing an interest in the company and changing form of management require a unanimous vote of the membership	• Articles of Organization must include the name "Limited Liability Company" or the initials "L.L.C" or "L.C." • Duration (if less than perpetual) • Name of Registered Agent in Arizona • Address of the Registered Office • Names and addresses of managers and members • A notice published in a newspaper of general circulation within 60 days of filing • Whether the company will be manager or member managed

ARKANSAS

Date of law	Status	Filing Fees	State Statute	Minimum Membership
April 12, 1993	Flexible	$50 filing fee $109 annual fee $25 name reserv	The Arkansas Small Business Entity Tax Pass Through Act of 93. ARK.CODE ANN.s.4-32-101to -1316	Arkansas recognizes single member LLCs

Foreign LLCs	Domestic LLCs	State Entity Tax	State Tax Classification	IRS Revenue Ruling
Recognized	Recognized	None	Arkansas follows federal income tax classifications	None

Required Records	Correspondence
• Names and addresses of all managers and members • Articles of Organization and amendments • All financial statements for three years • Current Operating Agreement	Secretary of State–Corporations Div. Aegon Building 501 Woodlane, Suite 310 Little Rock, AR 72201-1094 (501) 682-3409

Default Rules for LLC Operation	Requirements for Articles of Organization
• The company must be member managed • New members may be admitted only upon the unanimous vote of the membership • Any reduction in member's obligation to the company requires a unanimous vote of the membership • Professional LLCs are allowed	• Articles of Organization must include the name "Limited Liability Company" or the initials "L.L.C," "L.C.," "LLC" or "LC" • Duration (if not perpetual) • Name of Registered Agent in Arkansas • Registered Agent must acknowledge acceptance by signing the Articles • Address of Registered Office • Whether the company will be manager or member managed

CALIFORNIA

Date of law	Status	Filing Fees	State Statute	Minimum Membership
September 30, 1994	Flexible	$95	The California LLC Act CAL. CORP. CODE s. 17000 through s.17705	At least two members

Foreign LLCs	Domestic LLCs	State Entity Tax	State Tax Classification	IRS Revenue Ruling
Recognized	Recognized	$800 annual franchise tax and $400 gross receipts tax	California follows federal income tax classifications	94-6

Required Records	Correspondence
• Names and addresses of all managers and members • Articles of Organization and amendments • All financial statements for three years • Current Operating Agreement	Secretary of State 1500 11th Street, 6th Floor Sacramento, CA 95814 (916) 653-6814

Default Rules for LLC Operation	Requirements for Articles of Organization
• The LLC is member managed • Distributions are made on a *pro rata* basis • Any member can withdraw from the LLC upon 30 days written notice • Company may act upon unanimous vote of the membership • While member's interest is assignable, assignee may not participate in the management of the company	• Articles of Organization must include the name "Limited Liability Company" or the initials "L.L.C." The abbreviations "Ltd." and "Co." may also be used • Duration (if not perpetual) • Purpose of the company (may not be limited) • Name and address of the Registered Agent in California • Address of Registered Office • Whether the company will be manager or member managed

COLORADO

Date of law	Status	Filing Fees	State Statute	Minimum Membership
April 18, 1990 amended 1994	Bulletproof	$50 filing fee $25 annual fee $10 name reserv.	The Colorado LLC Act of 1990 COL.REV.STAT. s. 7-80-101 through 7-80-913	At least two members

Foreign LLCs	Domestic LLCs	State Entity Tax	State Tax Classification	IRS Revenue Ruling
Recognized	Recognized	None	All Colorado LLCs are treated as pass-through partnerships and must file partnership tax return	93-6

Required Records	Correspondence
• Names and addresses of all managers and members • Articles of Organization and amendments • All financial statements for three years • Current Operating Agreement • Minutes of every meeting	Secretary of State 1560 Broadway, Suite 200 Denver, CO 80202 (303) 894-2200

Default Rules for LLC Operation	Requirements for Articles of Organization
• The company may be manager or member managed • Only managers can incur a debt or liability in the LLCs name • Only cash distributions on a pro rata basis to members are allowed • Certified statement documenting each member's contribution and right of termination	• Articles of Organization must include the name "Limited Liability Company" or the initials "LLC" • Duration (not required by state) • Name of Registered Agent in Colorado • Address of Registered Office • Whether the company will be manager or member managed including names and addresses

CONNECTICUT

Date of law	Status	Filing Fees	State Statute	Minimum Membership
October 1, 1993	Flexible	$135	The Connecticut LLC Act Conn. Pub. Acts. 93-267	At least two members

Foreign LLCs	Domestic LLCs	State Entity Tax	State Tax Classification	IRS Revenue Ruling
Recognized	Recognized	None	Connecticut follows federal income tax classifications	None

Required Records	Correspondence
• Names and addresses of all present and past managers and members. • Articles of Organization and amendments • All financial statements for three years • Current Operating Agreement • All past Operating Agreements • Conditions of termination • Members' contributions to the company	Office of the Secretary of State State of Connecticut Corporations Division 30 Trinity Street Hartford, CT 06106 (860) 509-6000

Default Rules for LLC Operation	Requirements for Articles of Organization
• Distributions may be cash only and are made on a *pro rata* basis • Any member can withdraw from the LLC upon 30 days written notice • Any member who encumbers his interest does not surrender membership rights • A majority vote is necessary to admit a new member	• Articles of Organization must include the name "Limited Liability Company" or the initials "L.L.C." or "LLC." The abbreviations "Ltd." and "Co." may also be used. • Duration (if not perpetual) • Purpose of the company • Whether the company will be manager or member managed • Two copies of the Articles of Organization must be filed with the Secretary of State • The Organizing agent must sign the Articles of Organization and acknowledge receipt of appointment

DELAWARE

Date of law	Status	Filing Fees	State Statute	Minimum Membership
October 1, 1992 amended 1994 & 1995	Flexible	$72	The Delaware LLC Act DEL. CODE ANN. s. 18-101 through 18-1107	Only one person is required for formation

Foreign LLCs	Domestic LLCs	State Entity Tax	State Tax Classification	IRS Revenue Ruling
Recognized	Recognized	$100	Delaware follows federal income tax classifications	93-98

Required Records	Correspondence
Delaware does not require specific records be kept.	State of Delaware Division of Corporations P.O. Box 898 Dover, DE 19903 (302) 739-3073

Default Rules for LLC Operation	Requirements for Articles of Organization
• Profits and losses are allocated on a *pro rata* basis • Any member or manager can withdraw from the LLC upon 180 days notice • Bankruptcy, assignment for the benefit of creditors, and a court pleading for debtor protection will cause dissociation • Distributions to members must be made in cash and within a reasonable time • Members must honor their promised contributions to the company regardless of capacity to do so • Members may become creditors of an LLC • A member may assign his interest in the LLC • Assignee cannot participate in management of the LLC • Unless assignee is granted full membership in the LLC or authorized by LLC, he is not liable for liabilities of assignor • Mergers with all types of business entities are permitted • Within 90 days of a dissociative act, the LLC may continue if voted by the unanimous consent of remaining membership • Members have the right to access company records • One person may hold all of the offices of the LLC	• Articles of Organization must include the name "Limited Liability Company" or the initials "L.L.C." The name may contain the name of a member or manager. • Duration (not mandatory) • Purpose of the company • Name of Registered Agent in Delaware • Address of Registered Office • Operating Agreement must be in writing

DISTRICT OF COLUMBIA

Date of law	Status	Filing Fees	State Statute	Minimum Membership
July 23, 1994	Flexible	$45	The District of Columbia LLC Act D.C. CODE ANN. s. 29-1301 through s.29-1375	At least two members

Foreign LLCs	Domestic LLCs	State Entity Tax	State Tax Classification	IRS Revenue Ruling
Recognized	Recognized	10% tax on earned income	The District of Columbia follows federal income tax classifications	None

Required Records	Correspondence
• Names and addresses of all members • Articles of Organization and amendments • All financial statements for three years • Current Operating Agreement	Dept. of Consumer Reg. Affairs 614 "H" Street N.W., Rm 407 Washington, DC 20001 (202) 727-7278

Default Rules for LLC Operation	Requirements for Articles of Organization
• Profits and losses are allocated on a *pro rata* basis • Any member or manager can withdraw from the LLC upon 180 days notice • Distributions to members may be in cash if so demanded • Members must honor promised contributions the the LLC • A member may assign his interest in the LLC • The LLC shall be member managed • Actions taken by the LLC shall require at least the majority consent of the membership • No member or manager of the LLC shall have personal liability for debts or obligations of the LLC • In the event a member is unable to effect a promise to the LLC due to incapacity or death, the assignee of that membership may complete performance or forfeit assignor's membership interest	• Articles of Organization must include the name "Limited Liability Company" or the initials "L.L.C." • Duration (if less than perpetual) • Purpose of the company • Name of Registered Agent in the District of Columbia • Address of Registered Office • Names and addresses of initial membership • Conditions for admitting new members • Right to continue following dissolution or act of dissociation • Whether the company will be manager or member managed

FLORIDA

Date of law	Status	Filing Fees	State Statute	Minimum Membership
April 21, 1982	Bulletproof	$250 filing fee $35 fee for desig. of Regist. Agent	The Florida LLC Act FLA. STAT. ANN. s. 608.401 through s. 608.514	At least two members

Foreign LLCs	Domestic LLCs	State Entity Tax	State Tax Classification	IRS Revenue Ruling
Recognized	Recognized	5.5% artificial entity tax	Florida follows federal income tax classifications	93-53

Required Records	Correspondence
• Names and addresses of all members • Articles of Organization and amendments • All financial statements for three years • All federal, state, and local tax returns for three years • List of all member contributions	Division of Corporations P.O. Box 6327 Tallahassee, FL 32314 (850) 488-9000

Default Rules for LLC Operation	Requirements for Articles of Organization
• The LLC is member managed • All members are required to fulfill capital contribution obligations • A unanimous vote of the membership is required to admit new members • A member may withdraw upon providing 6 months written notice • A membership interest can only be assigned with the majority consent of the non-assigning members • An assignee can only become a member upon the unanimous approval of the membership	• Articles of Organization must include the name "Limited Liability Company", "Limited Company," the initials "L.L.C." or "L.C." • Duration (if less than perpetual) • Name of Registered Agent in Florida • Address of Registered Office • Whether the company will be manager or member managed and their names and addresses • Terms and conditions for admitting new members • Terms of continuation in the event of dissolution

GEORGIA

Date of law	Status	Filing Fees	State Statute	Minimum Membership
March 1, 1994	Flexible	$75 filing fee $109 annual fee $25 name reserv.	The Limited Liability Company Act. GA. CODE ANN. s. 14-11-1	Georgia recognizes single member LLCs

Foreign LLCs	Domestic LLCs	State Entity Tax	State Tax Classification	IRS Revenue Ruling
Recognized	Recognized	LLC must pay a 5% non-resident member withholding tax	Georgia follows federal income tax classifications	None

Required Records	Correspondence
• Names and addresses of all managers and members • Articles of Organization and amendments • All financial statements for three years • Current Operating Agreement	Secretary of State Corporations Department 2 Martin Luther King Junior Drive Suite 315, West Tower Atlanta, GA 30334 (404) 656-2817

Default Rules for LLC Operation	Requirements for Articles of Organization
• The company must be member managed • New members may be admitted only upon the unanimous vote of the membership • Georgia LLCs may not merge with corporations, but Georgia corporations may convert to LLCs • Membership interests are assignable • Unanimous consent of membership is required for an assignee to become a member • Any member may withdraw upon 6 months written notice	• Articles of Organization must include the name "Limited Liability Company" or "Limited Company," or the initials "L.L.C.," "L.C.," "LLC" or "LC." "Limited" and "Company" may be abbreviated "Ltd." and "Co." • Duration (if not perpetual) • Name of Registered Agent in Georgia • Whether the company will be manager or member managed

HAWAII

Date of law	Status	Filing Fees	State Statute	Minimum Membership
April 1, 1997	Flexible	$100 $25 name reservation	HIRST totle 23, Ch. 428 D.C. CODE ANN. s. 29-1301 through s.29-1375	One person

Foreign LLCs	Domestic LLCs	State Entity Tax	State Tax Classification	IRS Revenue Ruling
Recognized	Recognized	None		None

Required Records	Correspondence
	Dept. of Commerce & Consumer Affairs Business Registration Division P.O. Box 40 Honolulu, HI 96810 (808) 586-2744

Default Rules for LLC Operation	Requirements for Articles of Organization

	• Name of the company
	• Street address, U.S. post office box or rural post office number of original designated office
	• Name and address of initial agent for service of process
	• Name and address of each organizer
	• Duration of the company; if for a specified term, state the period specified
	• Whether the company is to be manager-managed, and:
	  • If so, names and addresses of each initial manager and the number of initial members; or
	  • If not, names and residence street addresses of each initial member
	• Whether members are liable for company debts and obligations under section 428-303(c)

IDAHO

Date of law	Status	Filing Fees	State Statute	Minimum Membership
July 1, 1993 amended 1994	Flexible	$100	The Idaho LLC Act IDAHO CODE s. 53-601	Idaho recognizes single member LCCs

Foreign LLCs	Domestic LLCs	State Entity Tax	State Tax Classification	IRS Revenue Ruling
Recognized	Recognized	None	Idaho follows federal income tax classifications	None

Required Records	Correspondence
• Names and addresses of all past and present managers and members • Articles of Organization and amendments • All financial statements for three years • Current Operating Agreement and amendments	Secretary of State P.O. Box 83720 Boise, ID 83720-0080 (208) 334-2300

Default Rules for LLC Operation	Requirements for Articles of Organization
• New members may be admitted only upon the unanimous vote of the membership • Membership interests are assignable • Unanimous consent of membership is required for new or assignee membership • Assignees may not participate in management • Any member may withdraw upon 30 days notice • An assignor loses his membership rights if his entire membership is assigned	• Articles of Organization must include the name "Limited Liability Company" or "Limited Company," or the initials "L.L.C.," "L.C." or "LC." "Limited" or "Company" may be abbreviated "Ltd." or "Co." • Duration (if not perpetual) • Name and address of Registered Agent in Idaho • Address of Registered Office • Whether the company will be manager or member managed

ILLINOIS

Date of law	Status	Filing Fees	State Statute	Minimum Membership
January 1, 1994	Flexible	$500 filing fee $300 annual fee $300 name reserv.	The Illinois LLC Act ILL. REV. STAT. ch 805 s. 180-1-10	At least two members

Foreign LLCs	Domestic LLCs	State Entity Tax	State Tax Classification	IRS Revenue Ruling
Recognized	Recognized	LLC is subject to a 1.5% partnership tax	Illinois follows federal income tax classifications	93-49

Required Records	Correspondence
• Names and addresses of all members and a list of their contributions • Date of each membership • Articles of Organization and amendments • All financial statements for three years • Current Operating Agreement and amendments	Secretary of State Department of Corporations 328 Howlett Building-Business Services Springfield, IL 62756 (217) 782-7880

Default Rules for LLC Operation	Requirements for Articles of Organization
• New members may be admitted only upon the unanimous vote of the membership • Membership interests in profits are assignable • A member may become a creditor of the LLC	• Articles of Organization must include the name "Limited Liability Company" or the initials "L.L.C." • Duration (if not perpetual) • Name and address of Registered Agent in Illinois • Address of Registered Office • Whether the company will be manager or member managed • Purpose of the company • Name and address of each organizer • Assumed name of the company, listed in the Articles of Organization

INDIANA

Date of law	Status	Filing Fees	State Statute	Minimum Membership
July 1, 1993	Flexible	$50	The Indiana Business Flexibility Act. IND. CODE s.23-18-1-1 through 23-18-13-1	At least two members

Foreign LLCs	Domestic LLCs	State Entity Tax	State Tax Classification	IRS Revenue Ruling
Recognized	Recognized	None	Indiana follows federal income tax classifications	None

Required Records	Correspondence
• Names and addresses of all managers and members • Articles of Organization and amendments • All financial statements and federal, state, and local tax returns for three years • Current Operating Agreement and amendments	Secretary of State-Corporation Division 302 W. Washington St., Rm E018 Indianapolis, IN 46204 (317) 232-6576

Default Rules for LLC Operation	Requirements for Articles of Organization
• New members including assignees may be admitted only upon the unanimous vote of the membership • Membership interests are assignable • LLCs may be member managed • Any member may, upon 30 days notice, withdraw from the LLC • Upon the unanimous vote of the membership, any member may be required to make a capital contribution or repay a distribution • Members have the right to remove an assignor • A member may receive any distribution in cash if so demanded • If the LLC has multiple managers, decisions are made by majority vote	• Articles of Organization must include the name "Limited Liability Company" or the initials "L.L.C." or "LLC" • Duration (if not perpetual) • Purpose of the company • Name and address of Registered Agent in Indiana • The business must be identified by the Standard Industrial Classification Code • Address of Registered Office • Whether the company will be manager or member managed

IOWA

Date of law	Status	Filing Fees	State Statute	Minimum Membership
July 1, 1992	Flexible	$50	The Iowa LLC Act IOWA CODE s. 490A.100 through 490A.1601	At least two members

Foreign LLCs	Domestic LLCs	State Entity Tax	State Tax Classification	IRS Revenue Ruling
Recognized	Recognized	None	Iowa follows federal income tax classifications	None

Required Records	Correspondence
• Names and addresses of all managers and members. • Articles of Organization and amendments • All financial statements and federal, state, and local tax returns for three years • Current Operating Agreement and amendments	Secretary of State-Corporation Division Hoover Blvd. 2nd Floor Des Moines, IA 50319 (515) 281-7563

Default Rules for LLC Operation	Requirements for Articles of Organization
• Assignees may be admitted only upon the unanimous vote of the membership • Membership interests are assignable • LLCs will be member managed • Managers must be elected with majority consent of the membership. • Membership, upon majority vote, may remove a manager with or without cause • Members vote based on percentage of ownership in LLC • Dissolution, winding up, transfer or encumbrance of all or substantially all of the LLC's assets, and amendments to the Articles of Organization or Operating Agreement must be with the unanimous consent of the membership • Managerial decisions must be made by majority vote • Members may, upon six months' notice, withdraw from the LLC • Members receive distributions on a *pro rata* basis	• Articles of Organization must include the name "Limited Liability Company" or the initials "L.C." • Duration (if not perpetual) • Name and Address of Registered Agent in Iowa • Address of Registered Office • Certificate of Registration must be filed by an organizer • Articles of Organization must be attached to the application

KANSAS

Date of law	Status	Filing Fees	State Statute	Minimum Membership
July 1, 1990	Flexible-Bulletproof	$150	The Kansas LLC Act KAN. STAT. ANN. s. 17-7610 through 17-7652	At least two members

Foreign LLCs	Domestic LLCs	State Entity Tax	State Tax Classification	IRS Revenue Ruling
Recognized	Recognized	Franchise tax	Kansas taxes LLCs as corporations	94-30

Required Records	Correspondence
• Names and addresses of all managers and members • Articles of Organization and amendments • All financial statements and federal, state, and local tax returns for three years • Copies of all minutes and business resolutions	Secretary of State Statehouse, 2nd Floor 300 SW 10th Street Topeka, KS 66612-1594 (913) 296-4564

Default Rules for LLC Operation	Requirements for Articles of Organization
• LLCs will be member managed, each member having one vote • The LLC may transact business with members • The Registered Agent and the Registered Office must have the same address • Dissolution occurs when a member unsuccessfully demands the return of his contribution • Financial information included in the annual report may be kept confidential • The Articles of Organization must contain the names and addresses of members if company is member managed • LLCs may not transact business until the Articles of Organization are filed • Members receive allocation or distributions on a *pro rata* basis	• Articles of Organization must include the name "Limited Liability Company," "Limited Company," or the initials "L.L.C.," "L.C.," "LLC" or "LC" • Duration (if not perpetual) • Name and address of Registered Agent in Kansas • Conditions for admission and rights of new members • Terms and conditions for continuing the company after dissociation • Whether the company will be manager or member managed • Address of Registered Office • Purpose of the company

KENTUCKY

Date of law	Status	Filing Fees	State Statute	Minimum Membership
March 29, 1994	Flexible	$40	The Kentucky LLC Act KY. REV. STAT. ANN. ch. 275 s.1 through s.93	At least two members

Foreign LLCs	Domestic LLCs	State Entity Tax	State Tax Classification	IRS Revenue Ruling
Recognized	Recognized	Franchise tax	Kentucky taxes LLCs as corporations	None

Required Records	Correspondence
• Names and addresses of all managers and members • Articles of Organization and amendments • All financial statements for five years and all federal, state, and local tax returns for three years • Current Operating Agreement and amendments	Secretary of State–Corporations Div. 152 Capitol Building 700 Capitol Avenue Frankfort, KY 40601 (502) 564-2848

Default Rules for LLC Operation	Requirements for Articles of Organization
• LLCs will be member managed • A membership interest is assignable • An assignee may not participate in the management of the company • Any new membership, including assignment, requires the unanimous consent of the membership • A member may withdraw upon 30 days' written notice • There will be only one class of membership • A majority vote (per capita) is necessary to approve action	• Articles of Organization must include the name "Limited Liability Company" or the initials "LLC" or "LC" • Duration (if not perpetual) • Name and address of Registered Agent in Kentucky • Address of Principal Office • Whether the company will be manager or member managed • Statement that there are at least two members

LOUISIANA

Date of law	Status	Filing Fees	State Statute	Minimum Membership
July 7, 1992	Flexible	$70 filing fee, $20 annual, $20 county, $210 name reserv.	The Louisiana LLC Act LA. REV. STAT. ANN. s.12:1301 through 12:1369	At least two members

Foreign LLCs	Domestic LLCs	State Entity Tax	State Tax Classification	IRS Revenue Ruling
Recognized	Recognized	None	Louisiana follows federal income tax classifications	94-5

Required Records	Correspondence
• Names and addresses of all managers and members • Articles of Organization and amendments • All financial statements and tax returns for three years • Current Operating Agreement	Secretary of State–Corporations Div. P.O. Box 94125 Baton Rouge, LA 70804-9125 (504) 925-4716

Default Rules for LLC Operation	Requirements for Articles of Organization
• The company may be member managed • Unless otherwise indicated, decisions are made by a majority vote of the managers, each having one vote • Absent a unanimous vote to the contrary, members are obligated to pay capital contributions even if incapacitated or dead • All distributions must be made in cash • Membership interests may be assigned or encumbered without loss of membership status • An assignee cannot participate in management without the unanimous consent of the membership • Profits will be equally allocated among members • LLCs may merge with other LLCs, partnerships or corporations • Voting is by a plurality of the membership • Managers may be removed without cause	• Articles of Organization must include the name "Limited Liability Company" or the initials "L.L.C." or "L.C." • Duration • The original and one copy of the Articles of Organization must be filed with the Secretary of State • The Registered Agent must acknowledge acceptance before a notary public • The organizers must file an initial report along with the Articles of Organization

MAINE

Date of law	Status	Filing Fees	State Statute	Minimum Membership
January 1, 1995	Flexible	$250 filing fee $60 annual fee	The Maine LLC Act ME. REV. STAT. ANN. titl. 31 s.601-762	Maine recognizes single-member LLCs

Foreign LLCs	Domestic LLCs	State Entity Tax	State Tax Classification	IRS Revenue Ruling
Recognized	Recognized	None	Maine follows federal income tax classifications	None

Required Records	Correspondence
• Names and addresses of all present and past managers and members • Articles of Organization and amendments • Current Operating Agreement	Secretary of State Department of Incorporation 101 State House Station Augusta, ME 04333-0101 (207) 287-6308

Default Rules for LLC Operation	Requirements for Articles of Organization
• Membership interests are assignable • Assignee has no right to participate in the management of the company • The LLC will be member managed • There is only one class of membership interest • The LLC is not under obligation to indemnify an agent or employee • Approval of action requires a majority vote of membership • Members vote on a *per capita* basis • Any member may withdraw from the LLC upon 30 days written notice • A unanimous vote is necessary to admit a new member	• Articles of Organization must include the name "Limited Liability Company" • Whether the company will be manager or member managed • Names and addresses of all managers of the LLC • Name and address of Registered Agent in Maine • Registered Agent must sign the Articles of Organization

MARYLAND

Date of law	Status	Filing Fees	State Statute	Minimum Membership
October 1, 1992	Flexible	$50	The Maryland LLC Act MD. CODE ANN. s. 4A-101 through s. 4A-1103	At least two members

Foreign LLCs	Domestic LLCs	State Entity Tax	State Tax Classification	IRS Revenue Ruling
Recognized	Recognized	5% withholding tax on non-resident members' distributive shares	Maryland LLCs must file a pass-through entity income tax return	None

Required Records	Correspondence
• Names and addresses of all members • Articles of Organization and amendments • All financial statements and tax returns for three years • Current Operating Agreement	State Dept. of Assess. and Tax. 301 W. Preston St., Room 809 Baltimore, MD 21201-2395 (410) 767-1340

Default Rules for LLC Operation	Requirements for Articles of Organization
• Membership interests are assignable • Assignee has no right to participate in the management of the company • The LLC can engage in business with its members • Members are agents of the LLC • Members vote on a *pro rata* basis • Members must make capital contributions to the LLC • If a dissociative event causes dissolution of the LLC, members may unanimously vote to continue the company • The LLC may assign its interests • A majority vote is necessary for management decisions • Any member may withdraw from the LLC upon six months' written notice • The Operating Agreement need not be in writing	• Articles of Organization must include the name "Limited Liability Company" or the initials "L.L.C.," "L.C.," "LLC" or "LC" • Purpose of the company • Name and address of Registered Agent in Maryland • Address of the Principal Office in Maryland

MASSACHUSETTS

Date of law	Status	Filing Fees	State Statute	Minimum Membership
January 1, 1996	Flexible	$500 filing fee, $500 annual, $15 name reserv.	The Massachusetts LLC Act MASS ACTS of 1995 ch. 281	At least two members

Foreign LLCs	Domestic LLCs	State Entity Tax	State Tax Classification	IRS Revenue Ruling
Recognized	Recognized	None	Massachusetts follows federal income tax classifications	None

Required Records	Correspondence
• Names and addresses of all members • Articles of Organization and amendments • All financial statements and tax returns for three years • Current Operating Agreement	Secretary of State Corporations Division State House Room 337 Boston, MA 02133 (617) 727-2853

Default Rules for LLC Operation	Requirements for Articles of Organization
• Membership interests are assignable • Assignee has no right to participate in the management of the company • The company shall be member managed • Members vote on a *pro rata* basis • Members must make capital contributions to the LLC • If a dissociative event causes dissolution of the LLC, members may unanimously vote to continue the company • The LLC may assign its interests • A majority vote in necessary for management decisions • Any member may withdraw from the LLC upon six months' written notice • The Operating Agreement need not be in writing • Professional LLCs are allowed	• Articles of Organization must include the name "Limited Liability Company," "Limited Company," or the initials "L.L.C.," "L.C.," "LLC" or "LC" • Duration • Purpose and nature of the company's business • Names and addresses of managers • Name and address of the Principal Agent in Massachusetts • Address of the Principal Office in Massachusetts

MICHIGAN

Date of law	Status	Filing Fees	State Statute	Minimum Membership
June 1, 1993	Flexible	$50	The Michigan LLC Act MICH. COMP. LAWS s.450.4101	At least two members

Foreign LLCs	Domestic LLCs	State Entity Tax	State Tax Classification	IRS Revenue Ruling
Recognized	Recognized	2.3% per year of the appropriate tax base	A Michigan LLC is subject to state income tax	None

Required Records	Correspondence
• Names and addresses of all managers and members • Articles of Organization and amendments • All financial statements and federal, state, and local tax returns for three years • Records outlining members' voting rights • Records of terms outlining ownership distributions	State of Michigan Dept of Commerce, Corp. Div. 6546 Mercantile Way Lansing, MI 48911 (517) 334-7561

Default Rules for LLC Operation	Requirements for Articles of Organization
• LLCs will be member managed, but manager(s) may be elected by a majority vote of the membership • Members are liable for contributions to the LLC • Managers may be terminated without cause • Any member may withdraw from the LLC upon 90 days' written notice • An assignee has no liability as a result of the assignment	• Articles of Organization must include the name "Limited Liability Company" or the initials "L.L.C." or "L.C." • Duration (may not be perpetual) • Name and of Registered Agent in Michigan • Names and addresses of the members • Whether the company will be manager or member managed • Address of Registered Office • Purpose of the company

MINNESOTA

Date of law	Status	Filing Fees	State Statute	Minimum Membership
January 1, 1993	Bulletproof	$135	The Minnesota LLC Act MINN. STAT. s. 322B.01	At least two members

Foreign LLCs	Domestic LLCs	State Entity Tax	State Tax Classification	IRS Revenue Ruling
Recognized	Recognized	None	Minnesota follows federal income tax classifications	None

Required Records	Correspondence
• Names and addresses of all managers and members • Articles of Organization and amendments • All financial statements and federal, state, and local tax returns for three years • Records outlining members' voting rights • Records of terms outlining ownership distributions • Current Operating Agreement	Secretary of State 100 Constitution Avenue, Rm 180 St. Paul, MN 55155-1299 (612) 215-1441

Default Rules for LLC Operation	Requirements for Articles of Organization
• The name of the LLC may not include the words "corporation" or "incorporated" • A Registered Agent is not required in Minnesota • The Registered Office may not be a post office box • Members vote on a *pro rata* basis • The organizers must sign the Articles of Organization • Profits and losses will be distributed to the members on *pro rata* basis	• Articles of Organization must include the name "Limited Liability Company" or the initials "L.L.C." • Duration (may not exceed 30 years) • Names and addresses of the members • Membership must appoint a chief manager and treasurer • Address of Registered Office • Business must be described in the Standard Industrial Classification Code • Name and address of each organizer • Terms of a continuation agreement in the event of dissolution

MISSISSIPPI

Date of law	Status	Filing Fees	State Statute	Minimum Membership
July 1, 1993	Flexible	$50	The Mississippi LLC Act MIS. CODE ANN. s. 79-29-101	Mississippi recognizes single-member LLCs

Foreign LLCs	Domestic LLCs	State Entity Tax	State Tax Classification	IRS Revenue Ruling
Recognized	Recognized	None	Mississippi follows federal income tax classifications	None

Required Records	Correspondence
• Names and addresses of all managers and members • Articles of Organization and amendments • Current Operating Agreement	Secretary of State Office of Incorporation P.O. Box 136 Jackson, MS 39205 (601) 359-1350

Default Rules for LLC Operation	Requirements for Articles of Organization
• LLCs are member managed but members may elect managers • Certificate of Formation must have a Federal Tax ID Number • A member may be a creditor of the LLC • Members have one vote each • Action taken by the LLC must be by majority vote • Any member may withdraw from the company upon 30 days' written notice • Distributions shall be made to membership on a *pro rata* basis • Profits and losses shall be allocated on a *pro rata* basis • The LLC shall indemnify any member or manager who successfully defends him or herself in a legal proceeding as a result of membership in the LLC • All distributions to members must be made in cash • A membership interest is assignable • A member loses his membership if his or her entire membership interest is assigned	• Articles of Organization must include the name "Limited Liability Company" or the initials "L.L.C." or "L.C." • Duration • Name and address of Registered Agent in Mississippi • Names and addresses of the members • Whether the company will be manager or member managed • Address of Registered Office

MISSOURI

Date of law	Status	Filing Fees	State Statute	Minimum Membership
December 1, 1993	Flexible	$105	The Missouri LLC Act MO. REV. STAT. S. 347.010 – 347.735	Missouri recognizes single-member LLCs

Foreign LLCs	Domestic LLCs	State Entity Tax	State Tax Classification	IRS Revenue Ruling
Recognized	Recognized	None	Missouri follows federal income tax classifications	None

Required Records	Correspondence
• Names and addresses of all managers and members • Articles of Organization and amendments • Current Operating Agreement • All financial statements and tax returns for three years • Records outlining members' voting rights • Records of terms outlining ownership distributions	Secretary of State–Corporations Div. P.O. Box 778 Jefferson City, MO 65102 (573) 751-1301

Default Rules for LLC Operation	Requirements for Articles of Organization
• Membership interests are assignable in whole or in part • A unanimous vote of the membership is required to admit a new member, approve a merger or consolidation, change the form of management, amend a member's contribution to the LLC, or engage in activity beyond the scope of the company • Distributions to members are made by majority vote • The LLC can engage in business with its members • Members may be creditors of the LLC	• Articles of Organization must include the name "Limited Liability Company" or the initials "L.L.C." or "L.C." • Purpose of the company • Name and address of Registered Agent in Missouri • Address of Registered Office • Name and address of each organizer • Terms for continuing in the event of dissociation of a member • Names and addresses of members • Conditions for admitting new members • Whether the company will be manager or member managed

MONTANA

Date of law	Status	Filing Fees	State Statute	Minimum Membership
October 1, 1993	Flexible	$70	The Montana LLC Act MONT. CODE ANN. s. 35-8-101	Montana recognizes single-member LLCs

Foreign LLCs	Domestic LLCs	State Entity Tax	State Tax Classification	IRS Revenue Ruling
Recognized	Recognized	None	Montana treats LLCs as partnerships	None

Required Records	Correspondence
• Names and addresses of all managers and members • Articles of Organization and amendments • All financial statements and tax returns for three years • Current Operating Agreement	Secretary of State P.O. Box 202801 Helena, MT 59620-2801 (406) 444-2034

Default Rules for LLC Operation	Requirements for Articles of Organization
• Professional LLCs are allowed but Articles of Organization must contain statement of services to be provided by the company • New members will be admitted to the LLC only upon the unanimous vote of the membership • A member's obligation can only be amended upon the unanimous vote of the membership • Members share equally in distributions after capital contributions are repaid by the company • Members must make capital contributions to the LLC • If a dissociative event causes dissolution of the LLC, members may unanimously vote to continue the company • The LLC may assign its interests • A majority vote is necessary for management decisions • Any member may withdraw from the LLC upon six months' written notice • The Operating Agreement need not be in writing	• Articles of Organization must include the name "Limited Liability Company," "Limited Company," or the initials "L.L.C.," "L.C.," "LLC" or "LC" • Name and address of Registered Agent in Montana • Whether the LLC will be manager or member managed • Address of the principal place of business • Names and addresses of members • Duration • Address of the Principal Office in Montana

176

NEBRASKA

Date of law	Status	Filing Fees	State Statute	Minimum Membership
September 9, 1993	Bulletproof	$100	The Nebraska LLC Act NEB. REV. STAT. s.21-2601	At least two members

Foreign LLCs	Domestic LLCs	State Entity Tax	State Tax Classification	IRS Revenue Ruling
Recognized	Recognized	None	Nebraska follows federal income tax classifications	None

Required Records	Correspondence
• Names and addresses of all managers and members • Articles of Organization and amendments • All financial statements and tax returns for three years • Current Operating Agreement	Secretary of State Corporate Division P.O. Box 94608 Lincoln, NB 68509 (402) 471-4079

Default Rules for LLC Operation	Requirements for Articles of Organization
• Members share assets on a *pro rata* basis. • No member may withdraw property from the LLC without consent of at least two-thirds of the membership • If a dissociative event causes dissolution of the LLC, members may, by at least a two-thirds vote, continue the company • The LLC may assign its interests	• Articles of Organization must include the name "Limited Liability Company" or the initials "L.L.C." • Name and address of Registered Agent in Nebraska • Whether the LLC will be manager or member managed • Names and addresses of members • Total contribution of each member • Terms and conditions for admitting new members • Terms and conditions for continuation following an act of dissolution • Duration (not to exceed 30 years) • Address of Principal Office in Nebraska

NEVADA

Date of law	Status	Filing Fees	State Statute	Minimum Membership
October 1, 1991	Bulletproof	$125 filing fee $85 annual fee	The Nevada LLC Act NEV. REV. STAT. s.86.011	At least two members

Foreign LLCs	Domestic LLCs	State Entity Tax	State Tax Classification	IRS Revenue Ruling
Recognized	Recognized	None	Franchise tax	94-30

Required Records	Correspondence
• Names and addresses of all managers and members • Articles of Organization and amendments • All financial statements and tax returns for three years • Current Operating Agreement	Secretary of State 101 N. Carson Street Carson City, NV 89701 (702) 687-5203

Default Rules for LLC Operation	Requirements for Articles of Organization
• Members share assets on a *pro rata* basis • Operating Agreement must be in writing • Executed Articles of Organization require verification • Members vote on *pro rata* basis • Members have the right to bind the company • Members may become creditors of the company	• Articles of Organization must include the name "Limited Liability Company" • Name and address of Registered Agent in Nevada • Provisions must be made for the return of members' contributions • Terms and conditions under which the company may continue in the event of dissociation • Duration (not to exceed 30 years) • Purpose of the company

NEW HAMPSHIRE

Date of law	Status	Filing Fees	State Statute	Minimum Membership
July 1, 1993	Flexible	$85	The New Hampshire Business Flexibility Act, N.H. REV. STAT. ANN. s.304-C:1 – s.304-C:85	At least two members

Foreign LLCs	Domestic LLCs	State Entity Tax	State Tax Classification	IRS Revenue Ruling
Recognized	Recognized	5% dividend tax, 7% on business profits	New Hampshire follows federal income tax classifications	None

Required Records	Correspondence
• Names and addresses of all managers and members • Articles of Organization and amendments • All financial statements and tax returns for three years • Current Operating Agreement	Secretary of State–Corporations Div. State House 107 Main Street, Room 204 Concord, NH 03301-4989 (603) 271-3246

Default Rules for LLC Operation	Requirements for Articles of Organization
• Name of the company may contain name of member or manager • Company may indemnify members of managers • Operating Agreement must be written • Business matters decided by majority vote of the membership • Membership interests may be assigned • Assignees do not incur liability as a result of the assignment • Professional LLCs are allowed in New Hampshire • The company is member managed	• Articles of Organization must include the name "Limited Liability Company" or the initials "L.L.C." • Name and address of Registered Agent in New Hampshire • Duration (not to exceed 30 years) • Names and addresses of members • Disclosure of any plans to sell membership interests as securities • Whether the company will be manager or member managed • Purpose of the company (recommended only)

NEW JERSEY

Date of law	Status	Filing Fees	State Statute	Minimum Membership
January 26, 1994	Flexible	$100	The New Jersey LLC Act N.J. REV. STAT. s.42	At least two members

Foreign LLCs	Domestic LLCs	State Entity Tax	State Tax Classification	IRS Revenue Ruling
Recognized	Recognized	None	New Jersey follows federal income tax classifications	None

Required Records	Correspondence
• Current Operating Agreement • Minutes of all member and manager meetings	Secretary of State P.O. Box 300 Trenton, NJ 08625 (609) 530-6431

Default Rules for LLC Operation	Requirements for Articles of Organization
• Members are liable for contributions to the company even if incapacitated • Company is member managed • Member obligations can be amended only with the unanimous consent of the membership • Any member may withdraw from the company upon six months written notice. • Operating Agreement must be written. • Prior to winding up or retirement, any member is entitled to receive distributions • After three years of improper distributions, a member is no longer liable	• Articles of Organization must include the name "Limited Liability Company" or the initials "L.L.C." • Name and address of Registered Agent in New Jersey • Duration (not to exceed 30 years) • Address of Registered Office

NEW MEXICO

Date of law	Status	Filing Fees	State Statute	Minimum Membership
June 17, 1993	Flexible	$50	The New Mexico LLC Act N.M. STAT. ANN. s.53-19-1	New Mexico recognizes single-member LLCs

Foreign LLCs	Domestic LLCs	State Entity Tax	State Tax Classification	IRS Revenue Ruling
Recognized	Recognized	None	New Mexico taxes LLCs as partnerships	None

Required Records	Correspondence
• None	State Corporation Commission P.O. Box 1269 Santa Fe, NM 87504-1269 (505) 827-4500

Default Rules for LLC Operation	Requirements for Articles of Organization
• Company is member managed • Managers or members decide by majority vote • If the company has perpetual existence, any member may withdraw from the company upon 30 days' written notice. • Registered Agent must accept appointment by signing an affidavit • Operating Agreement must be in writing • Unanimous consent of membership is necessary for removal of a member • New membership interests require the written consent of all members • An assignee can become a member upon the unanimous vote of the membership	• Articles of Organization must include the name "Limited Liability Company," "A Limited Company," or the initials "L.L.C.," "L.C.," "LLC" or "LC." The words "Limited" and "Company" may be abbreviated to "Ltd." and "Co." • Name and address of Registered Agent in New Mexico • Whether the company will be manager or member managed • Duration (if not perpetual) • Address of Registered Office

NEW YORK

Date of law	Status	Filing Fees	State Statute	Minimum Membership
October 23, 1994	Flexible	$200 filing fee; Notice of Publication costs up to $1800	The New York Limited Liability Law. Consolidated Laws of New York, Chapter 34	New York recognizes single-member LLCs

Foreign LLCs	Domestic LLCs	State Entity Tax	State Tax Classification	IRS Revenue Ruling
Recognized	Recognized	None	New York taxes LLCs at $50 per member, not to exceed $10,000	None

Required Records	Correspondence
• Names and addresses of all managers and members • Articles of Organization • Current Operating Agreement • All financial statements and tax returns for three years • Copies of all members' contributions, distributions and allocations	Secretary of State–Corporations Div. 41 State Street Albany, NY 12231 (518) 474-6200

Default Rules for LLC Operation	Requirements for Articles of Organization
• Company is member managed • Managers and members decide by majority vote • Any member may withdraw from the company upon six months' written notice • There may only be one class of members • Unanimous consent of membership is necessary for removal of a member • Any manager may be removed with the consent of the majority of the membership • The membership may, upon majority vote, continue the company after a terminating event • Professionals may form LLCs • New membership interests require the written consent of all members	• Articles of Organization must include the name "Limited Liability Company" or the initials "L.L.C." or "LLC" • Name and address of Registered Agent in New York • Whether the company will be manager or member managed • Statement authorizing Secretary of State to act as agent for service of process for the company • Statement of intention regarding members' liability for company debts • Duration (if not perpetual) • New LLCs must serve notice in two publications of general circulation, once a week for six successive weeks • Address of Principal Office

NORTH CAROLINA

Date of law	Status	Filing Fees	State Statute	Minimum Membership
October 1, 1993	Flexible	$100	The North Carolina LLC Act N.C. GEN. STAT. s.57c-1-101 through 57c-10-06	At least two members

Foreign LLCs	Domestic LLCs	State Entity Tax	State Tax Classification	IRS Revenue Ruling
Recognized	Recognized	None	North Carolina follows federal income tax classifications	None

Required Records	Correspondence
• Names and addresses of all members • Articles of Organization • All financial statements for five years • All federal, state, and local tax returns for five years • Current Operating Agreement and all amendments	Secretary of State–Corporations Div. 300 North Salisbury Street Raleigh, NC 27603-5909 (919) 733-4161

Default Rules for LLC Operation	Requirements for Articles of Organization
• The LLC is member managed • Members may agree to forbid withdrawals from the LLC prior to its dissolution • Members may receive only cash distributions • The LLC does not dissolve upon assignment • Unanimous vote of remaining membership required to admit assignee • Any member may withdraw from the company upon six months' written notice	• Articles of Organization must include the name "Limited Liability Company" or the initials "L.L.C." or "LLC." The words "Limited" and "Company" may be abbreviated to "Ltd." and "Co." • Duration (if less than perpetual) • Name and address of Registered Agent in North Carolina • Name and address of each organizer (at least two required)

NORTH DAKOTA

Date of law	Status	Filing Fees	State Statute	Minimum Membership
July 1, 1993	Flexible	$135	The North Dakota LLC Act N.D. CENT. CODE s.10-32-01 through 10-32-155	At least two members

Foreign LLCs	Domestic LLCs	State Entity Tax	State Tax Classification	IRS Revenue Ruling
Recognized	Recognized	None	North Dakota follows federal income tax classifications	None

Required Records	Correspondence
• Names and addresses of all members • Articles of Organization • List of all members' contributions • Minutes of all member meetings for the last three years • All financial statements for the last five years • All federal, state, and local tax returns for five years	Secretary of State–Corporations Div. 600 East Boulevard Avenue Bismark, ND 58505 (701) 328-4284

Default Rules for LLC Operation	Requirements for Articles of Organization
• The Operating Agreement need not be in writing • Each organizer must sign the Articles of Organization • Profits and losses will be allocated to members on a *pro rata* basis • Members vote on a *pro rata* basis	• Articles of Organization must include the name "Limited Liability Company" or the initials "L.L.C." • Duration (if less than perpetual) • Address of Principal Office • Name and address of Registered Agent in North Dakota • Registered Agent must agree to serve • Name and address of each organizer

OHIO

Date of law	Status	Filing Fees	State Statute	Minimum Membership
July 1, 1994	Flexible	$85	The Ohio LLC Act OHIO REV. CODE s. 1705.01 through 1705.58	At least two members

Foreign LLCs	Domestic LLCs	State Entity Tax	State Tax Classification	IRS Revenue Ruling
Recognized	Recognized	None	If the LLC is classified as an association, it will be treated as a corporation for income tax purposes	None

Required Records	Correspondence
• Names and addresses of all members • Articles of Organization and amendments • List of all members' contributions • All financial statements for three years • All federal, state, and local tax returns for three years • Copy of the Operating Agreement and all amendments	Secretary of State 30 East Broad Street, 14th Floor Columbus, OH 43266-0418 (614) 466-1145

Default Rules for LLC Operation	Requirements for Articles of Organization
• LLC will be member managed • An LLC membership interest may be exchanged for a promise to perform • Operating Agreement must be in writing • Members have management power based upon their percentage of ownership	• Articles of Organization must include the name "Limited Liability Company," "Limited," "Ltd." or "ltd" • Duration (if less than perpetual) • Address of Principal Office • Name, address and statement of acceptance of appointment of Registered Agent in Ohio • Operating Agreement must be in writing • Written statement of Registered Agent signed by a majority of membership

OKLAHOMA

Date of law	Status	Filing Fees	State Statute	Minimum Membership
September 1, 1992	Flexible-Bulletproof	$100	The Oklahoma LLC Act OKLA. STAT. ANN. s.2000	At least two members

Foreign LLCs	Domestic LLCs	State Entity Tax	State Tax Classification	IRS Revenue Ruling
Recognized	Recognized	None	Oklahoma follows federal income tax classifications	93-92

Required Records	Correspondence
• Names and addresses of all former and current managers and members • Articles of Organization • All financial statements for three years • All federal, state, and local tax returns for three years • Provisions for members' voting rights	Secretary of State 2300 N. Lincoln, Room 101 Oklahoma City, OK 73105 (405) 521-3911

Default Rules for LLC Operation	Requirements for Articles of Organization
• The Operating Agreement need not be in writing • At least one person must sign the Articles of Organization • Membership interest are assignable • Managers decide by majority vote • Assignee are not liable for assignor's liabilities • LLC will be managed by at least one manager	• Articles of Organization must include the name "Limited Liability Company," "Limited Company," or the initials "L.L.C." or "L.C." • Duration (if less than perpetual) • Address of Principal Office • Name and address of Registered Agent in Oklahoma

OREGON

Date of law	Status	Filing Fees	State Statute	Minimum Membership
January 4, 1994	Flexible	$140	The Oregon LLC Act OR. REV. STAT. s.63.01	Oregon recognizes single-member LLCs

Foreign LLCs	Domestic LLCs	State Entity Tax	State Tax Classification	IRS Revenue Ruling
Recognized	Recognized	None	Oregon follows federal income tax classifications	None

Required Records	Correspondence
• Names and addresses of all managers and members • Federal tax ID number • Address of Principal Business Office • Address of Registered Agent	Secretary of State Corporation Division 255 Capitol Street NE Salem, OR 97310-1327 (503) 986-2200

Default Rules for LLC Operation	Requirements for Articles of Organization
• The LLC will be member managed • A majority of the membership will elect the managers • Any member may withdraw from the company upon six months' notice • All membership distributions must be cash • Membership rights are assignable • Assignees are not liable for assignor's liabilities	• Articles of Organization must include the name "Limited Liability Company" or the initials "L.L.C." • Duration (if less than perpetual) • Purpose of the company • Whether the company will be manager or member managed • Name and address of each organizer • Name and address of Registered Agent in Oregon • Address of Principal Office

PENNSYLVANIA

Date of law	Status	Filing Fees	State Statute	Minimum Membership
February 6, 1995	Flexible	$45	The Pennsylvania LLC Act PA. CONS. STAT. v.15, ch.89	Pennsylvania recognizes single-member LLCs

Foreign LLCs	Domestic LLCs	State Entity Tax	State Tax Classification	IRS Revenue Ruling
Recognized	Recognized	Corporation tax	Pennsylvania taxes LLCs as corporations	None

Required Records	Correspondence
• Names and addresses of all members • Articles of Organization and any amendments • Current Operating Agreement	Commonwealth of Pennsylvania Corporations Office North Office Bldg., Room 302 Harrisburg, PA 17120 (717) 787-4057

Default Rules for LLC Operation	Requirements for Articles of Organization
• The LLC will be member managed • A majority of the membership or managers is necessary for decisions • Only one class of membership is allowed • Professional LLCs are permitted • New members may be admitted only upon majority vote of all members • An LLC may be divided into two LLCs • All members vote on a *per capita* basis • All managers may serve for either one year or until resignation, death or removal, whichever occurs first	• Articles of Organization must include the name "Limited Liability Company" or the initials "L.L.C." or "LLC" • Duration (if less than perpetual) • Purpose of the company • Name and address of Registered Agent in Pennsylvania • Names and addresses of members • Address of Registered Office • Whether the company will be manager or member managed

RHODE ISLAND

Date of law	Status	Filing Fees	State Statute	Minimum Membership
September 21, 1992	Flexible-Bulletproof	$150	The Rhode Island LLC Act R.I. GEN. LAWS s.7-16-1	At least two members

Foreign LLCs	Domestic LLCs	State Entity Tax	State Tax Classification	IRS Revenue Ruling
Recognized	Recognized	None	Rhode Island taxes LLCs as partnerships	93-81

Required Records	Correspondence
• Names and addresses of all managers and members • Articles of Organization and any amendments • All financial statements for five years • All federal, state, and local tax returns for five years	Secretary of State Corporations Office State House, Room 220 Providence, RI 02903 (401) 277-3040

Default Rules for LLC Operation	Requirements for Articles of Organization
• The Operating Agreement need not be in writing • Members vote on a *pro rata* basis • Profits and loss allocations will be made on a *pro rata* basis • Professional LLCs are not permitted	• Articles of Organization must include the name "Limited Liability Company" or the initials "L.L.C." or "LLC" • Duration (if not perpetual) • Purpose of the company • Name and address of Registered Agent in Rhode Island • Statement that there are at least two persons in the LLC • Address of Registered Office • Statement of tax treatment (whether partnership or corporate)

SOUTH CAROLINA

Date of law	Status	Filing Fees	State Statute	Minimum Membership
June 16, 1994	Flexible	$110	The South Carolina Limited Liability Act, S.C. CODE ANN. s.33-43-103	At least two members

Foreign LLCs	Domestic LLCs	State Entity Tax	State Tax Classification	IRS Revenue Ruling
Recognized	Recognized	None	South Carolina taxes LLCs as partnerships or corporations	None

Required Records	Correspondence
• Names and addresses of all managers and members • Articles of Organization and any amendments • All federal, state, and local tax returns for six years • Operating Agreement and amendments	Secretary of State P.O. Box 11350 Columbia, SC 29211 (803) 734-2158

Default Rules for LLC Operation	Requirements for Articles of Organization
• Company is member managed • Members may assign their interests • An assignee may not participate in management, nor have any participatory rights in the company including dissolution • An assignor does not lose membership rights • Unanimous consent of membership is necessary to amend a member's required contribution • New membership interests require the written consent of all members	• Articles of Organization must include the name "Limited Liability Company," "Limited Company," or the initials "L.L.C.," "L.C.," "LLC" or "LC." The words "Limited" and "Company" may be abbreviated to "Ltd." and "Co." • Name and address of Registered Agent in South Carolina • Whether the company will be manager or member managed • Names and signatures of the initial members • Duration (if not perpetual) • Address of Registered Office • Terms and conditions of winding up and dissolution • Value of each member's contributions and the conditions under which additional contributions will be required

SOUTH DAKOTA

Date of law	Status	Filing Fees	State Statute	Minimum Membership
July 1, 1993	Bulletproof	$50 and higher, depending upon initial capitalization	The South Dakota Limited Liability Act, S.D. CODIFIED LAWS, s.47-34-1	At least two members

Foreign LLCs	Domestic LLCs	State Entity Tax	State Tax Classification	IRS Revenue Ruling
Recognized	Recognized	None	No state income tax regardless of federal income tax classifications	95-9

Required Records	Correspondence
• Names and addresses of all managers and members • Articles of Organization and all amendments • All financial statements and federal, state, and local tax returns for past three years • Current Operating Agreement and all amendments	Secretary of State Attn: Corporations 500 E. Capitol, Suite 204 Pierre, SD 57501 (605) 773-4845

Default Rules for LLC Operation	Requirements for Articles of Organization
• Operating Agreement must be in writing • Company is member managed • The Articles of Organization must be signed in the presence of a notary by at least two members	• Articles of Organization must include the name "Limited Liability Company" or the initials "L.L.C." • Duration (if not perpetual) • Purpose of the company • Name and address of Registered Agent in South Dakota • Address of Registered Office • Whether the company will be manager or member managed • Terms for continuing the business after a dissociative event • Conditions for admission of new members • List of members' contributions

TENNESSEE

Date of law	Status	Filing Fees	State Statute	Minimum Membership
June 21, 1994	Flexible	$300 filing fee, $300 annual fee, $20 county record.	The Tennessee Limited Liability Act, TENN. CODE ANN. s.48A-1-101 through 48A-47-603	At least two members

Foreign LLCs	Domestic LLCs	State Entity Tax	State Tax Classification	IRS Revenue Ruling
Recognized	Recognized	$50 per member with annual cap of $3,000	Tennessee follows federal income tax classifications	None

Required Records	Correspondence
• Names and addresses of all managers and members • Articles of Organization and all amendments • All financial statements and federal, state, and local tax returns for past three years • Current Operating Agreement and all amendments • List of all assignees and the rights assigned • Records of all proceedings including management proceedings • Most recent LLC annual report	Secretary of State–Corporations Div. State Capitol, 1st Floor Nashville, TN 37243-0305 (615) 741-0529

Default Rules for LLC Operation	Requirements for Articles of Organization
• The LLC does not have the right to expel a member • If a company is member managed, any action requires the majority vote of the membership • The unanimous consent of remaining members is required to continue the company after a terminating event • Membership interest is not assignable; it is an act of dissociation • Professional LLCs are allowed • There may be only one class of membership	• Articles of Organization must include the name "Limited Liability Company" or the initials "L.L.C." or "LLC" • Name and address of Registered Agent in Tennessee • Duration (if not perpetual) • Address of Principal Office • Statement indicating that there are at least two members at time of filing • Name and address of each organizer • Whether the company will be manager or member managed

TEXAS

Date of law	Status	Filing Fees	State Statute	Minimum Membership
August 26, 1992	Flexible	$200	The Texas LLC Act TEX. REV. CIV. STAT. ANN. art.1528n	Texas recognizes single-member LLCs

Foreign LLCs	Domestic LLCs	State Entity Tax	State Tax Classification	IRS Revenue Ruling
Recognized	Recognized	25% of capital and 4.5% of earned surplus	Texas levies a franchise tax on LLCs	None

Required Records	Correspondence
• Names and addresses of all managers and members • Articles of Organization and any amendments • All federal, state, and local tax returns for six years • List of members' contributions	Secretary of State–Corporations Div. P.O. Box 13697 Austin, TX 78711-3697 (512) 463-5586

Default Rules for LLC Operation	Requirements for Articles of Organization
• Company is member managed • Managers need not be residents of Texas • New members may be admitted only by unanimous written consent of all members • There may be only one class of membership • The organizer must sign the Articles of Incorporation • New membership interests require the written consent of all members	• Articles of Organization must include the name "Limited Liability Company," "Limited Company," or the initials "L.L.C.," "L.C.," "LLC" or "LC." The words "Limited" and "Company" may be abbreviated to "Ltd." and "Co." • Name and address of Registered Agent in Texas • Name and address of each organizer • Names and addresses of all managers and members • Purpose of the company • Duration (if not perpetual) • Address of Registered Office

UTAH

Date of law	Status	Filing Fees	State Statute	Minimum Membership
July 1, 1991 amended in 1992 and 1994	Flexible	$50	The Utah LLC Act UTAH CODE ANN. s.48-2b-102	At least two members

Foreign LLCs	Domestic LLCs	State Entity Tax	State Tax Classification	IRS Revenue Ruling
Recognized	Recognized	None	Utah follows federal income tax classifications	93-91

Required Records	Correspondence
• Names and addresses of all managers and members • Articles of Organization and any amendments • All financial statements and federal, state, and local tax returns for three years • List of members' contributions	Department of Commerce P.O. Box 146791 Salt Lake City, UT 84114-6701 (801) 530-6027

Default Rules for LLC Operation	Requirements for Articles of Organization
• Company is member managed • Company may continue following a dissolution event only if all members consent within 90 days of the event • New members may be admitted only by unanimous written consent of all members • Registered Agent must sign an acknowledgement form • Distributions need not be made in cash • Members have the authority to bind the LLC • Operating Agreement need not be in writing • Operating Agreement may include a provision outlining conditions for terminating a member's interest	• Articles of Organization must include the name "Limited Liability Company," "Limited Company," or the initials "L.L.C.," "L.C.," "LLC" or "LC" • Name and address of Registered Agent in Utah • Name and address of each organizer • Names and addresses of all managers and members • Purpose of the company • Signature of Registered Agent plus signature of at least two members or managers • Duration (if not perpetual) • Address of Registered Office

VERMONT

Date of law	Status	Filing Fees	State Statute	Minimum Membership
July 1, 1996	Flexible	$75	The Vermont Limited Liability Act, V. St. Title 11 Ch. 21 S 3001-3162	One person

Foreign LLCs	Domestic LLCs	State Entity Tax	State Tax Classification	IRS Revenue Ruling
Recognized	Recognized	None		None

Required Records	Correspondence
None	Secretary of State Corporations Division 109 State Street Montpelier, VT 05609-1101 (802) 828-2386

Default Rules for LLC Operation	Requirements for Articles of Organization
	• Articles of Organization must include the name "Limited Liability Company," "Limited Company," or the initials "L.L.C.," "LLC," "L.C.," or "LC" • Name of the company • Address of the initial designated office • Name and street address of initial agent for service of process • Name and address of each organizer • Whether the company is to be manager-managed, and if so the name and address of each initial manager • Whether members of the company are to be liable for debts and obligations under subsection (b) of section 3043 of this title

VIRGINIA

Date of law	Status	Filing Fees	State Statute	Minimum Membership
July 1, 1991	Bulletproof	$100	The Virginia Limited Liability Act, VA. CODE ANN. s.13.1-1073	At least two members

Foreign LLCs	Domestic LLCs	State Entity Tax	State Tax Classification	IRS Revenue Ruling
Recognized	Recognized	None	Virginia follows federal income tax classifications	None

Required Records	Correspondence
• Names and addresses of all managers and members • Articles of Organization and all amendments • All financial statements and federal, state, and local tax returns for three years • Operating Agreement for past three years	Commonwealth of Virginia State Corporation Commission P.O. Box 1197 Richmond, VA 23218 (804) 371-9376

Default Rules for LLC Operation	Requirements for Articles of Organization
• Operating Agreement does not have to be in writing • The Registered Agent must be a member, manager, or attorney • Liability of members or managers for duty of care is limited to the greater of $100,000 or amount of compensation paid during the 12 months preceding the act • Company is manager managed • Members may remove a manager without cause • The statutory terms for continuation of the company in the event of a termination event may not be altered by the Operating Agreement	• Articles of Organization must include the name "Limited Liability Company" or the initials "L.L.C." or "L.C." • Name and of Registered Agent in Virginia • Signature of Organizer(s) • Duration (if not perpetual) • Address of Principal Office • Address of Registered Office

WASHINGTON

Date of law	Status	Filing Fees	State Statute	Minimum Membership
October 1, 1994	Flexible	$175	The Washington Limited Liability Act, WASH. REV. CODE s.25.15	At least two members

Foreign LLCs	Domestic LLCs	State Entity Tax	State Tax Classification	IRS Revenue Ruling
Recognized	Recognized	None	Washington taxes LLCs as partnerships	None

Required Records	Correspondence
• Names and addresses of all current and former managers and members • Articles of Organization and all amendments • All financial statements and federal, state, and local tax returns for three years • Operating Agreement and all amendments • List of members' contributions	Secretary of State Corporation Division P.O. Box 40220 Olympia, WA 98504-0220 (360) 753-2896

Default Rules for LLC Operation	Requirements for Articles of Organization
• Any member may withdraw from the LLC upon 30 days' written notice • The Registered Agent must be a member of an active Washington corporation, LLC or limited partnership, or a resident of the state • Members and managers have limited liability • Company is member managed • All financial relationships between the LLC and its members shall be in writing • Any assignee is entitled to receive distributions from LLC • Any member may be a creditor of the LLC • Registered Agent must sign a consent to be appointed form • Registered Agent must have the same address as the Principal Office • Professional LLCs are permitted • Upon assignment of membership interest, the assignor loses that interest and is no longer a member of the LLC • Business affairs of the LLC shall be decided by a majority consent of the membership	• Articles of Organization must include the name "Limited Liability Company," "Limited Company," or the initials "L.L.C." The word "Company" may be abbreviated "Co." • Name and address of Registered Agent in Washington • Whether the company will be manager or member managed • Duration (if not perpetual) • Address of Principal Office • Names and addresses of persons executing the Articles of Organization

WEST VIRGINIA

Date of law	Status	Filing Fees	State Statute	Minimum Membership
March 6, 1992	Bulletproof	$10	The West Virginia Limited Liability Act, W. VA. CODE s.31-1A-1 through s.31-1-1A-69	At least two members

Foreign LLCs	Domestic LLCs	State Entity Tax	State Tax Classification	IRS Revenue Ruling
Recognized	Recognized	None	West Virginia follows federal income tax classifications	93-50

Required Records	Correspondence
• None	Secretary of State–Corporations Div. 1900 Kanawha Boulevard E Building 1, Suite 157-K Charleston, WV 25305-0770 (304) 558-8000

Default Rules for LLC Operation	Requirements for Articles of Organization
• Operating Agreement does not have to be in writing • LLC will be member managed • Management vacancies will be filled by a majority vote of the membership • Upon majority vote of members, managers may be removed without cause • Any member may withdraw from the LLC upon six months' written notice	• Articles of Organization must include the name "Limited Liability Company" • Duration (if less than perpetual) • Purpose of the company • Name and address of Registered Agent in West Virginia • Address of Principal Office • Names and addresses of initial members • Name and address of Organizer(s) must be included in the Articles of Organization • Signature of authorized person

WISCONSIN

Date of law	Status	Filing Fees	State Statute	Minimum Membership
January 1, 1994	Flexible	$90	The Wisconsin Limited Liability Act, WIS. STAT. chapter 183	At least two members

Foreign LLCs	Domestic LLCs	State Entity Tax	State Tax Classification	IRS Revenue Ruling
Recognized	Recognized	Possible temporary surcharge if taxed as a partnership	Wisconsin follows federal income tax classifications	None

Required Records	Correspondence
• Names and addresses of all managers and members • Articles of Organization and all amendments • All financial statements and federal, state, and local tax returns for three years • Operating Agreement and all amendments • LLC's records must be kept at the Principal Office	Department of Financial Institutions Corporations and Consumer Division P.O. Box 7846 Madison, WI 53707-7846 (608) 261-9550

Default Rules for LLC Operation	Requirements for Articles of Organization
• Membership interests may be assigned • Assignees may become members upon the unanimous vote of the membership • The Operating Agreement must be in writing	• Articles of Organization must include the name "Limited Liability Company" or the initials "L.L.C." or "LLC." The word "Company" may be abbreviated "Co." • Name and address of Registered Agent in Wisconsin • Whether the company will be manager or member managed • Name of the person drafting the Articles of Organization • Statement of intent to be taxed as a partnership for federal income tax purposes • Address of the Principal Office • Names and addresses of members

WYOMING

Date of law	Status	Filing Fees	State Statute	Minimum Membership
1997	Flexible	$100 filing fee $150 annual fee	The Wyoming Limited Liability Act, WYO. STAT. s.17-15-101 through 17-15-136	At least two members

Foreign LLCs	Domestic LLCs	State Entity Tax	State Tax Classification	IRS Revenue Ruling
Recognized	Recognized	None	No state tax	88-76

Required Records	Correspondence
• None	Secretary of State Corporations Division State Capitol Bldg. Cheyenne, WY 82002-0020 (307) 777-7314

Default Rules for LLC Operation	Requirements for Articles of Organization
• Membership interests may be assigned • Assignees may become members upon the unanimous vote of the membership • The Operating Agreement must be in writing • The LLC does not dissolve upon assignment • Members may bind the company if there are no managers • Managers may bind the company only if so authorized	• Articles of Organization must include the name "Limited Liability Company" or the initials "L.L.C." or "LLC." The word "Company" may be abbreviated "Co." • Duration (limited to 30 years) • Purpose of the company • Name and address of Registered Agent in Wyoming • Address of Registered Office • The conditions upon which the company may continue after a terminating event • Terms and conditions for admitting new members • Whether the company will be manager or member managed • List of members' contributions • Names and addresses of members

How to save on attorney fees

How to save on attorney fees

Millions of Americans know they need legal protection, whether it's to get agreements in writing, protect themselves from lawsuits, or document business transactions. But too often these basic but important legal matters are neglected because of something else millions of Americans know: legal services are expensive.

They don't have to be. In response to the demand for affordable legal protection and services, there are now specialized clinics that process simple documents. Paralegals help people prepare legal claims on a freelance basis. People find they can handle their own legal affairs with do-it-yourself legal guides and kits. Indeed, this book is a part of this growing trend.

When are these alternatives to a lawyer appropriate? If you hire an attorney, how can you make sure you're getting good advice for a reasonable fee? Most importantly, do you know how to lower your legal expenses?

When there is no alternative

Make no mistake: serious legal matters require a lawyer. The tips in this book can help you reduce your legal fees, but there is no alternative to good professional legal services in certain circumstances:

- when you are charged with a felony, you are a repeat offender, or jail is possible

- when a substantial amount of money or property is at stake in a lawsuit

- when you are a party in an adversarial divorce or custody case

- when you are an alien facing deportation

- when you are the plaintiff in a personal injury suit that involves large sums of money

- when you're involved in very important transactions

Are you sure you want to take it to court?

Consider the following questions before you pursue legal action:

What are your financial resources?

Money buys experienced attorneys, and experience wins over first-year lawyers and public defenders. Even with a strong case, you may save money by not going to court. Yes, people win millions in court. But for every big winner there are ten plaintiffs who either lose or win so little that litigation wasn't worth their effort.

Do you have the time and energy for a trial?

Courts are overbooked, and by the time your case is heard your initial zeal may have grown cold. If you can, make a reasonable settlement out of court. On personal matters, like a divorce or custody case, consider the emotional toll on all parties. Any legal case will affect you in some way. You will need time away from work. A newsworthy case may bring press coverage. Your loved ones, too, may face publicity. There is usually good reason to settle most cases quickly, quietly, and economically.

How can you settle disputes without litigation?

Consider *mediation*. In mediation, each party pays half the mediator's fee and, together, they attempt to work out a compromise informally. *Binding arbitration* is another alternative. For a small fee, a trained specialist serves as judge, hears both sides, and hands down a ruling that both parties have agreed to accept.

So you need an attorney

Having done your best to avoid litigation, if you still find yourself headed for court, you will need an attorney. To get the right attorney at a reasonable cost, be guided by these four questions:

What type of case is it?

You don't seek a foot doctor for a toothache. Find an attorney experienced in your type of legal problem. If you can get recommendations from clients who have recently won similar cases, do so.

Where will the trial be held?

You want a lawyer familiar with that court system and one who knows the court personnel and the local protocol—which can vary from one locality to another.

Should you hire a large or small firm?

Hiring a senior partner at a large and prestigious law firm sounds reassuring, but chances are the actual work will be handled by associates—at high rates. Small firms may give your case more attention but, with fewer resources, take longer to get the work done.

What can you afford?

Hire an attorney you can afford, of course, but know what a fee quote includes. High fees may reflect a firm's luxurious offices, high-paid staff and unmonitored expenses, while low estimates may mean "unexpected" costs later. Ask for a written estimate of all costs and anticipated expenses.

How to find a good lawyer

Whether you need an attorney quickly or you're simply open to future possibilities, here are seven nontraditional methods for finding your lawyer:

1) **Word of mouth**: Successful lawyers develop reputations. Your friends, business associates and other professionals are potential referral sources. But beware of hiring a friend. Keep the client-attorney relationship strictly business.

2) **Directories**: The Yellow Pages and the Martin-Hubbell Lawyer Directory (in your local library) can help you locate a lawyer with the right education, background and expertise for your case.

3) **Databases**: A paralegal should be able to run a quick computer search of local attorneys for you using the Westlaw or Lexis database.

4) **State bar associations**: Bar associations are listed in phone books. Along with lawyer referrals, your bar association can direct you to low-cost legal clinics or specialists in your area.

5) **Law schools**: Did you know that a legal clinic run by a law school gives law students hands-on experience? This may fit your legal needs. A third-year law student loaded with enthusiasm and a little experience might fill the bill quite inexpensively—or even for free.

6) **Advertisements**: Ads are a lawyer's business card. If a "TV attorney" seems to have a good track record with your kind of case, why not call? Just don't be swayed by the glamour of a high-profile attorney.

7) **Your own ad**: A small ad describing the qualifications and legal expertise you're seeking, placed in a local bar association journal, may get you just the lead you need.

How to hire and work with your attorney

No matter how you hear about an attorney, you must interview him or her in person. Call the office during business hours and ask to speak to the attorney directly. Then explain your case briefly and mention how you obtained the attorney's name. If the attorney sounds interested and knowledgeable, arrange for a visit.

The ten-point visit

1) Note the address. This is a good indication of the rates to expect.

2) Note the condition of the offices. File-laden desks and poorly maintained work space may indicate a poorly run firm.

3) Look for up-to-date computer equipment and an adequate complement of support personnel.

4) Note the appearance of the attorney. How will he or she impress a judge or jury?

5) Is the attorney attentive? Does the attorney take notes, ask questions, follow up on points you've mentioned?

6)   Ask what schools he or she has graduated from, and feel free to check credentials with the state bar association.

7)   Does the attorney have a good track record with your type of case?

8)   Does he or she explain legal terms to you in plain English?

9)   Are the firm's costs reasonable?

10)   Will the attorney provide references?

Hiring the attorney

Having chosen your attorney, make sure all the terms are agreeable. Send letters to any other attorneys you have interviewed, thanking them for their time and interest in your case and explaining that you have retained another attorney's services.

Request a letter from your new attorney outlining your retainer agreement. The letter should list all fees you will be responsible for as well as the billing arrangement. Did you arrange to pay in installments? This should be noted in your retainer agreement.

Controlling legal costs

Legal fees and expenses can get out of control easily, but the client who is willing to put in the effort can keep legal costs manageable. Work out a budget with your attorney. Create a timeline for your case. Estimate the costs involved in each step.

Legal fees can be straightforward. Some lawyers charge a fixed rate for a specific project. Others charge contingency fees (they collect a percentage of your recovery, usually 35-50 percent if you win and nothing if you lose). But most attorneys prefer to bill by the hour. Expenses can run the gamut, with one hourly charge for taking depositions and another for making copies.

Have your attorney give you a list of charges for services rendered and an itemized monthly bill. The bill should explain the service performed, who performed the work, when the service was provided, how long it took, and how the service benefits your case.

Ample opportunity abounds in legal billing for dishonesty and greed. There is also plenty of opportunity for knowledgeable clients to cut their bills significantly if they know what to look for. Asking the right questions and setting limits on fees is smart and can save you a bundle. Don't be afraid to question legal bills. It's your case and your money!

When the bill arrives

- **Retainer fees**: You should already have a written retainer agreement. Ideally, the retainer fee applies toward case costs, and your agreement puts that in writing. Protect yourself by escrowing the retainer fee until the case has been handled to your satisfaction.

- **Office visit charges**: Track your case and all documents, correspondence, and bills. Diary all dates, deadlines and questions you want to ask your attorney during your next office visit. This keeps expensive office visits focused and productive, with more accomplished in less time. If your attorney charges less for phone consultations than office visits, reserve visits for those tasks that must be done in person.

- **Phone bills**: This is where itemized bills are essential. Who made the call, who was spoken to, what was discussed, when was the call made, and how long did it last? Question any charges that seem unnecessary or excessive (over 60 minutes).

- **Administrative costs**: Your case may involve hundreds, if not thousands, of documents: motions, affidavits, depositions, interrogatories, bills, memoranda, and letters. Are they all necessary? Understand your attorney's case strategy before paying for an endless stream of costly documents.

- **Associate and paralegal fees**: Note in your retainer agreement which staff people will have access to your file. Then you'll have an informed and efficient staff working on your case, and you'll recognize their names on your bill. Of course, your attorney should handle the important part of your case, but less costly paralegals or associates may handle routine matters more economically. Note: Some firms expect their associates to meet a quota of billable hours, although the time spent is not always warranted. Review your bill. Does the time spent make sense for the document in question? Are several staff involved in matters that should be handled by one person? Don't be afraid to ask questions. And withhold payment until you have satisfactory answers.

- **Court stenographer fees**: Depositions and court hearings require costly transcripts and stenographers. This means added expenses. Keep an eye on these costs.

- **Copying charges**: Your retainer fee should limit the number of copies made of your complete file. This is in your legal interest, because multiple files mean multiple chances others may access your confidential information. It is also in your financial interest, because copying costs can be astronomical.

- **Fax costs**: As with the phone and copier, the fax can easily run up costs. Set a limit.

- **Postage charges**: Be aware of how much it costs to send a legal document overnight, or a registered letter. Offer to pick up or deliver expensive items when it makes sense.

- **Filing fees**: Make it clear to your attorney that you want to minimize the number of court filings in your case. Watch your bill and question any filing that seems unnecessary.

- **Document production fee**: Turning over documents to your opponent is mandatory and expensive. If you're faced with reproducing boxes of documents, consider having the job done by a commercial firm rather than your attorney's office.

- **Research and investigations**: Pay only for photographs that can be used in court. Can you hire a photographer at a lower rate than what your attorney charges? Reserve that right in your retainer agreement. Database research can also be extensive and expensive; if your attorney uses Westlaw or Nexis, set limits on the research you will pay for.

- **Expert witnesses**: Question your attorney if you are expected to pay for more than a reasonable number of expert witnesses. Limit the number to what is essential to your case.

- **Technology costs**: Avoid videos, tape recordings, and graphics if you can use old-fashioned diagrams to illustrate your case.

- **Travel expenses**: Travel expenses for those connected to your case can be quite costly unless you set a maximum budget. Check all travel-related items on your bill, and make sure they are appropriate. Always question why the travel is necessary before you agree to pay for it.

- **Appeals costs**: Losing a case often means an appeal, but weigh the costs involved before you make that decision. If money is at stake, do a cost-benefit analysis to see if an appeal is financially justified.

- **Monetary damages**: Your attorney should be able to help you estimate the total damages you will have to pay if you lose a civil case. Always consider settling out of court rather than proceeding to trial when the trial costs will be high.

- **Surprise costs**: Surprise costs are so routine they're predictable. The judge may impose unexpected court orders on one or both sides, or the opposition will file an unexpected motion that increases your legal costs. Budget a few thousand dollars over what you estimate your case will cost. It usually is needed.

- **Padded expenses**: Assume your costs and expenses are legitimate. But some firms do inflate expenses—office supplies, database searches, copying, postage, phone bills—to bolster their bottom line. Request copies of bills your law firm receives from support services. If you are not the only client represented on a bill, determine those charges related to your case.

Keeping it legal without a lawyer

The best way to save legal costs is to avoid legal problems. There are hundreds of ways to decrease your chances of lawsuits and other nasty legal encounters. Most simply involve a little common sense. You can also use your own initiative to find and use the variety of self-help legal aid available to consumers.

11 situations in which you may not need a lawyer

1) **No-fault divorce**: Married couples with no children, minimal property, and no demands for alimony can take advantage of divorce mediation services. A lawyer should review your divorce agreement before you sign it, but you will have saved a fortune in attorney fees. A marital or family counselor may save a seemingly doomed marriage, or help both parties move beyond anger to a calm settlement. Either way, counseling can save you money.

2) **Wills**: Do-it-yourself wills and living trusts are ideal for people with estates of less than $600,000. Even if an attorney reviews your final documents, a will kit allows you to read the documents, ponder your bequests, fill out sample forms, and discuss your wishes with your family at your leisure, without a lawyer's meter running.

3) **Incorporating**: Incorporating a small business can be done by any business owner. Your state government office provides the forms and instructions necessary. A visit to your state office will probably be

necessary to perform a business name check. A fee of $100-$200 is usually charged for processing your Articles of Incorporation. The rest is paperwork: filling out forms correctly; holding regular, official meetings; and maintaining accurate records.

4) **Routine business transactions**: Copyrights, for example, can be applied for by asking the U.S. Copyright Office for the appropriate forms and brochures. The same is true of the U.S. Patent and Trademark Office. If your business does a great deal of document preparation and research, hire a certified paralegal rather than paying an attorney's rates. Consider mediation or binding arbitration rather than going to court for a business dispute. Hire a human resources/benefits administrator to head off disputes concerning discrimination or other employee charges.

5) **Repairing bad credit**: When money matters get out of hand, attorneys and bankruptcy should not be your first solution. Contact a credit counseling organization that will help you work out manageable payment plans so that everyone wins. It can also help you learn to manage your money better. A good company to start with is the Consumer Credit Counseling Service, 1-800-388-2227.

6) **Small Claims Court**: For legal grievances amounting to a few thousand dollars in damages, represent yourself in Small Claims Court. There is a small filing fee, forms to fill out, and several court visits necessary. If you can collect evidence, state your case in a clear and logical presentation, and come across as neat, respectful and sincere, you can succeed in Small Claims Court.

7) **Traffic Court**: Like Small Claims Court, Traffic Court may show more compassion to a defendant appearing without an attorney. If you are ticketed for a minor offense and want to take it to court, you will be asked to plead guilty or not guilty. If you plead guilty, you can ask for leniency in sentencing by presenting mitigating circumstances. Bring any witnesses who can support your story, and remember that presentation (some would call it acting ability) is as important as fact.

8) **Residential zoning petition**: If a homeowner wants to open a home business, build an addition, or make other changes that may affect his or her neighborhood, town approval is required. But you don't need a lawyer to fill out a zoning variance application, turn it in, and present your story at a public hearing. Getting local support before the hearing is the best way to assure a positive vote; contact as many neighbors as possible to reassure them that your plans won't adversely affect them or the neighborhood.

9) **Government benefit applications**: Applying for veterans' or unemployment benefits may be daunting, but the process doesn't require legal help. Apply for either immediately upon becoming eligible. Note: If your former employer contests your application for unemployment benefits and you have to defend yourself at a hearing, you may want to consider hiring an attorney.

10) **Receiving government files**: The Freedom of Information Act gives every American the right to receive copies of government information about him or her. Write a letter to the appropriate state or federal agency, noting the precise information you want. List each document in a separate paragraph. Mention the Freedom of Information Act, and state that you will pay any expenses. Close with your signature and the address the documents should be sent to. An approved request may take six months to arrive. If it is refused on the grounds that the information is classified or violates another's privacy, send a letter of appeal explaining why the released information would not endanger anyone. Enlist the support of your local state or federal representative, if possible, to smooth the approval process.

11) **Citizenship**: Arriving in the United States to work and become a citizen is a process tangled in bureaucratic red tape, but it requires more perseverance than legal assistance. Immigrants can learn how to obtain a "Green Card," under what circumstances they can work, and what the requirements of citizenship are by contacting the Immigration Services or reading a good self-help book.

Save more; it's E-Z

When it comes to saving attorneys' fees, E-Z Legal Forms is the consumer's best friend. America's largest publisher of self-help legal products offers legally valid forms for virtually every situation. E-Z Legal Kits and E-Z Legal Guides include all necessary forms with a simple-to-follow manual of instructions or a layman's book. E-Z Legal Books are a legal library of forms and documents for everyday business and personal needs. E-Z Legal Software provides those same forms on disk and CD for customized documents at the touch of the keyboard.

You can add to your legal savvy and your ability to protect yourself, your loved ones, your business and your property with a range of self-help legal titles available through E-Z Legal Forms. See the product descriptions and information at the back of this guide.

E·Z LEGAL® SOFTWARE

AS EASY AS 1,2,3!

1 Loads from 3.5" disk or CD, both included.

2 Just click on a form title to open it.
E-Z category menu and dialog box help you find the form you need.

3 Print professional forms in minutes.

Vital Record Keeping Made E-Z*
Over 200 ready-to-use forms to organize every aspect of your life, from business and finance to health and recreation.

3.5 disks only.

Item No. SW306

Accounting–Deluxe Edition
The fastest, most economical accounting system for your small business. It handles every accounting function and is ideal for any type of business.

Item No. SW1123

W-2 Maker
Saves valuable time during tax season. Quickly, accurately and easily completes stacks of W-2s, W-3s, 1099s, 1096s and more. Perfect for accounting departments.

Item No. SW1147

Buying/Selling Your Home Made E-Z
Buy or sell almost any property with forms for listings, deeds, offers, mortgages, agreements and closing—plus helpful legal and financial tips.

Item No. SW1111

E-Z Construction Estimator
Every Contractor can profit from this time-saving software. It automatically calculates the detailed costs of a given project, from equipment to labor.

Item No. CD316

Financial Forecaster
The fast way to protect your financial future and make informed decisions. Easily calculate changes to your mortgage, investments, annuities, income and more!

Item No. SW1122

* Only $14.95 each for *Family Record Organizer and Last Will & Testament*

E·Z LEGAL® SOFTWARE

...when you need it in writing!®

E-Z Legal Software, 384 S. Military Trail, Deerfield Beach, FL 33442
(800) 822-4566 • fax: (954) 480-8906
web site: http://www.e-zlegal.com

Designed for
Microsoft
Windows 95

Microsoft, Windows, Windows NT, and the Windows logo are registered trademarks of Microsoft Corporation.

ss 1999.r1

BE INFORMED — BE PROTECTED!

The E-Z Legal Sexual Harassment Poster

If you do not have a well-communicated sexual harassment policy, you are vulnerable to employee lawsuits for sexual harassment.

Give your employees the information they need and protect your company from needless harassment suits by placing this poster wherever you hang your labor law poster.

BONUS! Receive our helpful manual *How to Avoid Sexual Harassment Lawsuits* with your purchase of the Sexual Harassment Poster.

See the order form in this guide, and order yours today!

FEDERAL & STATE
Labor Law Posters

The Poster 15 Million Businesses Must Have This Year!

All businesses must display federal labor laws at each location, or risk fines and penalties of up to $7,000!
And changes in September and October of 1997 made all previous Federal Labor Law Posters obsolete;
so make sure you're in compliance—use ours!

State	Item#
Alabama	83801
Alaska	83802
Arizona	83803
Arkansas	83804
California	83805
Colorado	83806
Connecticut	83807
Delaware	83808
Florida	83809
Georgia	83810
Hawaii	83811
Idaho	83812
Illinois	83813
Indiana	83814
Iowa	83815
Kansas	83816
Kentucky	83817

State	Item#
Louisiana	83818
Maine	83819
Maryland	83820
Massachusetts	83821
Michigan	83822
Minnesota	83823
Mississippi	83824
Missouri	83825
Montana	83826
Nebraska	83827
Nevada	83828
New Hampshire	83829
New Jersey	83830
New Mexico	83831
New York	83832
North Carolina	83833
North Dakota	83834

State	Item#
Ohio	83835
Oklahoma	83836
Oregon	83837
Pennsylvania	83838
Rhode Island	83839
South Carolina	83840
South Dakota not available	
Tennessee	83842
Texas	83843
Utah	83844
Vermont	83845
Virginia	83846
Washington	83847
Washington, D.C.	83848
West Virginia	83849
Wisconsin	83850
Wyoming	83851

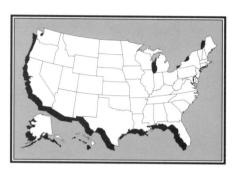

State Labor Law Compliance Poster

Avoid up to $10,000 in fines by posting the required State Labor Law Poster available from E-Z Legal.

$29.95

Federal Labor Law Poster

This colorful, durable 17³/₄" x 24" poster is in full federal compliance and includes:

- The NEW Fair Labor Standards Act Effective October 1, 1996 (New Minimum Wage Act)
- The Family & Medical Leave Act of 1993*
- The Occupational Safety and Health Protection Act of 1970
- The Equal Opportunity Act
- The Employee Polygraph Protection Act

Businesses with fewer than 50 employees should display reverse of poster, which excludes this act.

$11.99
Stock No. LP001

ss1999.r1

See the order form in this guide to order yours today!

E•Z Legal Kits	Item#	Qty.	Price Ea.
Bankruptcy	K100		$21.95
Incorporation	K101		$21.95
Divorce	K102		$27.95
Credit Repair	K103		$18.95
Living Trust	K105		$18.95
Living Will	K106		$21.95
Last Will & Testament	K107		$16.95
Small Claims Court	K109		$19.95
Traffic Court	K110		$19.95
Buying/Selling Your Home	K111		$18.95
Employment Law	K112		$18.95
Collecting Child Support	K115		$18.95
Limited Liability Company	K116		$18.95

E•Z Legal Software			
Everyday Legal Forms & Agreements Made E-Z	CD311		$29.95
Managing Employees Made E-Z	CD312		$29.95
Corporate Record Keeping Made E-Z	CD314		$29.95
E-Z Construction Estimator	CD316		$29.95
Incorporation Made E-Z	SW1101		$29.95
Divorce Law Made E-Z	SW1102		$29.95
Credit Repair Made E-Z	SW1103		$29.95
Living Trusts Made E-Z	SW1105		$29.95
Last Wills Made E-Z	SW1107		$14.95
Buying/Selling Your Home Made E-Z	SW1111		$29.95
W-2 Maker	SW1117		$14.95
Asset Protection Secrets Made E-Z	SW1118		$29.95
Solving IRS Problems Made E-Z	SW1119		$29.95
Everyday Law Made E-Z	SW1120		$29.95
Vital Record Keeping Made E-Z	SW306		$14.95

E•Z Legal Books			
Family Record Organizer	BK300		$24.95
301 Legal Forms & Agreements	BK301		$24.95
Personnel Director	BK302		$24.95
Credit Manager	BK303		$24.95
Corporate Secretary	BK304		$24.95
Immigration (English/Spanish)	BK305		$24.95
E-Z Legal Advisor	LA101		$24.95

Made E•Z Guides			
Bankruptcy Made E-Z	G200		$17.95
Incorporation Made E-Z	G201		$17.95
Divorce Law Made E-Z	G202		$17.95
Credit Repair Made E-Z	G203		$17.95
Living Trusts Made E-Z	G205		$17.95
Living Wills Made E-Z	G206		$17.95
Last Wills Made E-Z	G207		$17.95
Small Claims Court Made E-Z	G209		$17.95
Traffic Court Made E-Z	G210		$17.95
Buying/Selling Your Home Made E-Z	G211		$17.95
Employment Law Made E-Z	G212		$17.95
Trademarks & Copyrights Made E-Z	G214		$17.95
Collecting Child Support Made E-Z	G215		$17.95
Limited Liability Companies Made E-Z	G216		$17.95
Partnerships Made E-Z	G218		$17.95
Solving IRS Problems Made E-Z	G219		$17.95
Asset Protection Secrets Made E-Z	G220		$17.95
Immigration Made E-Z	G223		$17.95
Managing Personnel Made E-Z	G223		$17.95
Corporate Record Keeping Made E-Z	G223		$17.95
Vital Record Keeping Made E-Z	G223		$17.95
Buying/Selling a Business Made E-Z	G223		$17.95
Business Forms Made E-Z	G223		$17.95
Collecting Unpaid Bills Made E-Z	G223		$17.95
Everyday Law Made E-Z	G223		$17.95
Everyday Legal Forms & Agreements Made E-Z	G223		$17.95

Labor Posters			
Federal Labor Law Poster	LP001		$11.99
State Labor Law Poster (specify state)			$29.95
Sexual Harassment Poster	LP003		$ 9.95
SHIPPING & HANDLING*			$
TOTAL OF ORDER**:			$

ss 1999.1

See an item in this book you would like to order?

To order :
1. Photocopy this order form.
2. Use the photocopy to complete your order and mail to:

E•Z LEGAL FORMS®

384 S Military Trail, Deerfield Beach, FL 33442
phone: (954) 480-8933 • fax: (954) 480-8906
web site: http://www.e-zlegal.com/

Shipping and Handling: **Add $3.50 for the first item, $1.50 for each additional item.**

Florida residents add 6% sales tax.

Total payment must accompany all orders.
Make checks payable to: E•Z Legal Forms, Inc.

NAME

COMPANY

ORGANIZATION

ADDRESS

CITY   STATE   ZIP

PHONE (   )

PAYMENT:

❑ **CHECK ENCLOSED, PAYABLE TO E-Z LEGAL FORMS, INC.**

❑ **PLEASE CHARGE MY ACCOUNT:** ❑ MasterCard ❑ VISA   EXP.DATE

ACCOUNT NO.

Signature: _____
(required for credit card purchases)

-OR-

For faster service, order by phone:
(954) 480-8933

Or you can fax your order to us:
(954) 480-8906

Index

A-I ✦✦✦✦

L-C ✦✦✦✦